COMPREHENSIVE RESEARCH
AND STUDY GUIDE

Walt Whitman

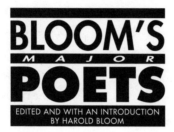

EDITED AND WITH AN INTRODUCTION
BY HAROLD BLOOM

Walt
Whitman

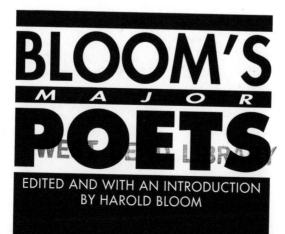

BLOOM'S *MAJOR* POETS

EDITED AND WITH AN INTRODUCTION
BY HAROLD BLOOM

© 1999 by Chelsea House Publishers, a division of Main Line Book Co.

Introduction © 1999 by Harold Bloom

Printed and bound in the United States of America.

First Printing
1 3 5 7 9 8 6 4 2

Library of Congress Cataloging-in-Publication Data
Walt Whitman / edited and with an introduction by Harold Bloom.
cm.—(Bloom's major poets) 440
Includes bibliographical references and index.
ISBN 0-7910-5108-0 (hc)
Whitman, Walt, 1819-1892—Criticism and interpretation—
Handbooks, manuals, etc. 2. Whitman, Walt, 1819-1892—
Examinations—Study guides. I. Bloom, Harold. II. Series.
PS3238.W354   1998
811.'3—dc21   98-4339
CIP

Chelsea House Publishers
1974 Sproul Road, Suite 400
Broomall, PA 19008-0914

Contributing Editor: Janyce Marsen

Contents

User's Guide

This volume is designed to present biographical, critical, and bibliographical information on the author's best-known or most important poems. Following Harold Bloom's editor's note and introduction is a detailed biography of the author, discussing major life events and important literary accomplishments. A thematic and structural analysis of each poem follows, tracing significant themes, patterns, and motifs in the work.

A selection of critical extracts, derived from previously published material from leading critics, analyzes aspects of each poem. The extracts consist of statements from the author, if available, early reviews of the work, and later evaluations up to the present. A bibliography of the author's writings (including a complete list of all books written, cowritten, edited, and translated), a list of additional books and articles on the author and the work, and an index of themes and ideas in the author's writings conclude the volume.

〜

Harold Bloom is Sterling Professor of the Humanities at Yale University and Henry W. and Albert A. Berg Professor of English at the New York University Graduate School. He is the author of over 20 books and the editor of more than 30 anthologies of literary criticism.

Professor Bloom's works include *Shelley's Mythmaking* (1959), *The Visionary Company* (1961), *Blake's Apocalypse* (1963), *Yeats* (1970), *A Map of Misreading* (1975), *Kabbalah and Criticism* (1975), and *Agon: Toward a Theory of Revisionism* (1982). *The Anxiety of Influence* (1973) sets forth Professor Bloom's provocative theory of the literary relationships between the great writers and their predecessors. His most recent books include *The American Religion* (1992), *The Western Canon* (1994), *Omens of Millennium: The Gnosis of Angels, Dreams, and Resurrection* (1996), and *Shakespeare: The Invention of the Human* (1998).

Professor Bloom earned his Ph.D. from Yale University in 1955 and has served on the Yale faculty since then. He is a 1985 MacArthur Foundation Award recipient and served as the Charles Eliot Norton Professor of Poetry at Harvard University in 1987–88. He is currently the editor of other Chelsea House series in literary criticism, including BLOOM'S NOTES, BLOOM'S MAJOR SHORT STORY WRITERS, MAJOR LITERARY CHARACTERS, MODERN CRITICAL VIEWS, MODERN CRITICAL INTERPRETATIONS, and WOMEN WRITERS OF ENGLISH AND THEIR WORKS.

Editor's Note

My Introduction, an overview of Walt Whitman's major poems, centers upon his highly original psychic cartography, which is still little understood.

Since the Critical Views are numerous, I will cite only a few here. John T. Irwin, exuberant both as critic and as poet, strikingly characterizes *Leaves of Grass* as a "hieroglyphic Bible," a work of Edenic childhood.

Gay Wilson Allen and Charles T. Davis present the familial context of "As I Ebb'd with the Ocean of Life," after which Paul Zweig deepens the context.

Whitman's biographer Justin Kaplan, broods on the relation between the nature writer John Burroughs and Whitman's great elegy for President Lincoln, "When Lilacs Last in the Dooryard Bloom'd," while Charles Feidelson discusses the poem's symbolism.

The feminist critic Sandra Gilbert sees "Out of the Cradle Endlessly Rocking" as a "gender-inflected structure." Carol Z. Whalen invokes Julia Kristeva as an aid to reading "The Sleepers," while R. W. French finds a model for the poem in traditional dream-visions.

Mutlu Blasing very acutely analyzes the concept of the self in "The Sleepers," while Roger Asselineau describes images of time in "Crossing Brooklyn Ferry," and Susan Strom usefully compares Whitman's "face to face" confrontation with the flood-tide, in that poem, to Jacob's struggle with the Angel (or perhaps God) in Genesis.

Introduction

HAROLD BLOOM

Walt Whitman is, in every good sense, our national poet, and *Leaves of Grass* is the essential American book: the poems of our climate. Cultural fashions vary, and the Whitman of our moment sometimes seems to be celebrated and studied only as an exemplary instance of "the Homosexual Poetic." Though doubtless homoerotic in his yearnings, Whitman's poetic stance is fiercely universal, and pervasively autoerotic. This may have some relation to the declared prophetic and religious purpose of the poetry. Whitman astonishingly audacious, proclaims himself as the American Christ. That will shock many among us, and is the true scandal of the author of "Song of Myself." In the notebook where "Song of Myself" finds its origin, the earliest draft of what will become section 38 remains a surprise to us:

> In vain were nails driven through my hands.
> I remember my crucifixion and bloody coronation
> I remember the mockers and the buffeting insults
> The sepulchre and the white linen have yielded me up
> I am alive in New York and San Francisco,
> Again I tread the streets after two thousand years.
> Not all the traditions can put vitality in churches
> They are not alive, they are cold mortar and brick,
> I can easily build as good, and so can you:—
> Books are not men—

Of the Crucifixion, Emerson had remarked: "This was a Great Defeat, but we demand Victory." "We" meant Americans, for whom Jesus is not so much the sufferer on the cross but the man of the Resurrection, who wandered about with his disciples for forty days and nights before the Ascension. That is the Whitman of the final fifteen sections of "Song of Myself," the resurrected American Jesus:

> I remember now,
> I resume the overstaid fraction,
> The grave of rock multiplies what has been confided to it, or to
> any graves,
> Corpses rise, gashes heal, fastening roll from me.

Greeting the 1855 *Leaves of Grass* in his letter to Whitman, Emerson wonderfully observed: "I am very happy in reading it, as great power makes me happy." *Power* is the precise word, the potency or potential for more life. Walt Whitman incarnates power in its best sense, which is the power to vitalize others. His great poem of Incarnation is "The Sleepers," a Night Vision in which he begins the extraordinary process of identification that will ensue in the mergings of night, death, the mother, and the sea, a fusion bequeathed by Whitman to much subsequent American poetry.

"Song of Myself," a difficult internalized epic still too little understood, manifests its strongest originality in Whitman's psychic cartography, which had few precedents and has had few analogues since, whether in the literature or the psychologies of the Twentieth century, Freudian psychoanalysis included. Whitman found three components in consciousness, which he termed the soul, the self, and "the real ME" or "me myself." By the soul, Whitman meant character, as opposed to the self or personality. What Whitman regarded as his darker aspect, an estranged or alienated element in his nature, his soul, which comes out of the depths in most of his major poems. But his central poem is called "Song of Myself," and not "Song of My Soul." By "myself," Whitman means what he calls "Walt Whitman, an American, one of the roughs." Yet that more masculine or aggressive part of the self is split from "the real Me" or "me myself," which ultimately is one with the world of night, death, the mother, and the sea. Though the Whitmanian soul is blank and professedly unknown to him, the "real Me" is something like a knowing even as one is known, a kind of American Gnosis, of which Whitman is an authentic seer.

Whitman primarily intended to celebrate his poetic self, but even his most expansive apprehensions in "Song of Myself" are shadowed by "the spirit that trails in the lines underfoot," the spirit of "As I Ebb'd with the Ocean of Life" and "When Lilacs Last in the Dooryard Bloom'd." Rather unwillingly, Whitman became the great American elegist, lamenting the fall of the poetic self:

> I too but signify at the utmost a little wash'd-up drift,
> A few sands and dead leaves to gather,
> Gather, and merge myself as part of the sands and drift.

For me, the strongest of all Whitman's poems is "When Lilacs Last in the Dooryard Bloom'd." Here, counting "the tally of my soul," Whitman supremely hymns his unknown soul through its emblem, the hermit thrush:

In the swamp in secluded recesses,
A shy and hidden bird is warbling a song.

Solitary the thrush,
The hermit withdrawn to himself, avoiding the settlements,
Sings by himself a song.

At the close of "Song of Myself," Whitman achieves his most per-
suasive affirmation:

You will hardly know who I am or what I mean,
But I shall be good health to you nevertheless,
And filter and fibre your blood.
Failing to fetch me at first keep encouraged,
Missing me one place search another,
I stop somewhere waiting for you.

He speaks of our relation, as readers, to him, but this seems to me
also the true song of his unknown soul, and can be taken as
addressed to his self or selves. Out of the maelstrom of his consciousness, Whitman created the most vital and vitalizing art yet to
appear in what he called "these states," the "shores of America" to
which, as he affirmed, Emerson had led him. ❀

Biography of
Walt Whitman

(1819–1873)

In 1855, having just read the newly published volume of poems *Leaves of Grass*, Ralph Waldo Emerson wrote to Walt Whitman, its author, congratulating him "at the beginning of a great career, which must have had a long foreground somewhere, for such a start." Indeed, Emerson was so impressed with Whitman's poetic achievement that he is reported to have said that here was proof of an American Buddha, a national poet. And that, truly, was Whitman's final aspiration—to acquire a national identity and become the acknowledged American prophet—an aspiration that was the impetus behind his life's work in both his poetry and his active engagement in the political and social issues of his day. Walt Whitman did indeed see himself as a public spokesman and a social healer, an orator whose public voice would enable him to assume the dual role of poet and caretaker.

For Walt Whitman, the pursuit of health was the supreme good. Whitman would be forever boasting of his excellent health in *Leaves of Grass*. "I, now thirty-seven years old in perfect health begin,/ Hoping to cease not till death." In fact, Whitman was a cultural repository for many of the popular health "sciences" of his day. These concerns grew out of Whitman's interest in phrenology, the belief that the conformations of the skull are indicative of mental faculties and character; animal magnetism, which sought to bridge mind and matter, claiming to cure disease and extend life; and hydropathy, or the "water cure," a big business in New York in the 1840s and—despite its larger schemes promising social and individual happiness—actually produced some important changes in the hygienic habits of the times.

Walt Whitman was born on May 31, 1819, the second of eight children, to a Long Island farmer and his wife. The family soon moved to Brooklyn during a building boom. Although undistinguished himself, Walter, the poet's father, was acquainted with some of the powerful personalities of his day, including the American revolutionist and political philosopher Thomas Paine and the eloquent, outspoken Quaker orator Elias Hicks. Leaving school at the age of eleven, Whitman immediately went to work as an office boy in a law firm. At this time, he was also already enamored of the romantic novels of Sir Walter Scott, one of the writers who was to give rise to his rich imagination.

By fifteen, Whitman was on his own, frequently crossing the ferry from Brooklyn to attend debating societies and the theater. Whitman began his career in journalism around this time, until a fire in 1835 disrupted the printing business in New York. For five years thereafter, he taught intermittently at country and small-town schools.

In 1838, Whitman started his own newspaper. By the time he was 23, Whitman had become the editor of the *Aurora*, a Manhattan daily, and wrote regularly about the eccentricities of city life. His daily routine of purposeless walks, in which he could revel in the sights and sounds of the city, afforded him the opportunity to take daily swims and visit the local bathhouses regularly. After a while, the *Aurora* fired him, accusing him of laziness. Shortly thereafter, Whitman traveled to New Orleans, his only extensive trip until much later in life.

Once back in New York, Whitman became profoundly influenced by a group of Brooklyn artists and frequented the opera, where he heard the great Italian prima donna Marietta Alboni. At this time he was living with his family again in Brooklyn, ignoring regular meal-times and loafing away the day in walks, reading libraries, and a writing room that he shared with his brother. He became a student of astronomy and Egyptology and gleaned articles out of the great British magazines, developing very definite opinions about pantheism, a doctrine that holds that the universe *conceived of as a whole* is God.

Walt Whitman printed and published the first edition of *Leaves of Grass* in 1855. On the frontispiece he placed an engraving of himself as a bearded laborer, shirt open at the neck, right arm akimbo and left arm in his pocket—an image that hardly bespeaks a man who would be reading verse, much less writing it. His prefatory essay to *Leaves of Grass* was likewise bold and daring, focusing on the sort of poet he thought America required and the kind of poetry that America could expect from him. "The American poets are to enclose old and new for America is the race of races. Of them a bard is to be commensurate with a people."

Whitman's father died shortly after the initial publication of *Leaves of Grass,* and he was left to support his mother and a mentally retarded brother. At first there were only a few reviews, so Whitman anonymously published some of his own; he even attached clippings of Emerson's famous congratulatory letter to copies he presented to his friends. Successive editions of *Leaves of Grass* appeared until 1892, the year of the last edition; these celebrate such themes as the love of man for woman, to counterbalance his strong sentiments regarding the love of men for men. There is also a movement in the later editions, according to Whitman's biographer Gay Wilson Allen, toward greater theoretical and philosophical issues.

Whitman was a nurse during the Civil War. He went to Washington, D.C., in 1862 to care for his wounded brother George and stayed on to help as many of the ailing soldiers as he could. Following a gradual decline in his reputation and the paralytic stroke he suffered in 1873, Whitman left Washington to return to Brooklyn. After his mother's death a few months later, Whitman moved to Camden, New Jersey, to live with his brother George. Isolated from the intellectual stimulation of his friends, his convalescence was a lonely experience.

The 1876 edition of *Leaves of Grass,* published for the American centennial, caught the attention of such English writers as Alfred, Lord Tennyson. This brought in much-needed funds and caused the American public to take notice that the invalid poet, virtually ignored in his own country, was achieving international acclaim.

Whitman died in Camden on March 26, 1892, with the knowledge and satisfaction that he remained true to himself and his art. Before his death he commissioned a mausoleum, a plain, massive temple of unpolished granite, to be erected upon a twenty-by-thirty-foot plot of land. ❀

Thematic Analysis of
"Song of Myself"

Leaves of Grass, the general title for Whitman's complete volume of poems, underwent ten different sets of revisions and additions between 1855 and 1892, with the 1855 edition setting forth the poet's manifesto that "the United States themselves are essentially the greatest poem" and that as their national bard, his poetic spirit "incarnates its geography and natural life."

The 1855 edition is dominated by the inaugural poem. Untitled in the 1855 edition, in 1856 it became "A Poem of Walt Whitman, an American"; in the 1881 edition it received the title by which it is known today. "Song of Myself" is written in free verse—a self-conscious and deliberately unstructured form of poetry consisting of long lines, often mixing verse with song. It is a composite of all the ideas that preoccupied Whitman throughout his life and his writing. The title places the poem within two fundamental contexts: autobiography and epic poetry, the ancient tradition of oral poetry in which the poet, or "bard," sings the story of a hero's trials and victories. An epic poem is an extended narrative written in poetic language that sets forth the story of a people or a nation; in a sense, it is a national history, to be memorialized and handed down through generations. In "Song of Myself," Whitman names—and praises—Americans in all walks of life and grants them "divine" status through the combined grandeur of body and soul.

In "Song of Myself," Whitman establishes a poetic identity that is uniquely American, a poetic form that breaks with the old forms and dry subject matter inherited from the long, extensive British literary tradition. As the opening stanza states, Whitman is the hero singing his own song of self-congratulation:

> I celebrate myself, and sing myself,
> And what I assume you shall assume,
> For every atom belonging to me as good belongs to you.

He speaks for America and identifies himself with all:

> I am of old and young, of the foolish as much as the wise,
> Regardless of others, ever regardful of others,
> Maternal as well as paternal, a child as well as a man.

Within this democratic society, embracing every social and ethnic group living together in harmony, Whitman champions individual freedom and expression, evidenced throughout the poem in his descriptions and "cataloguing" of details. The poetic "I" is the creator of this new poetry for a new America; Whitman establishes the primacy of his own voice as the spiritual guide and healer. The ubiquitous "I" does not represent the poet's conventional speaking voice. Rather, as Harold Bloom explains it, the real "me" of the poem is a divided self, consisting of "my self," "my soul," and the "me myself," none of which can be clearly pinned down.

Whitman presents himself as the ever-present hero, healthy and strong:

> I, now thirty-seven years old in perfect health begin

and establishes himself as the fighter for all causes:

> I am the mate and champion of people, all just as immortal and
> fathomless as myself.

He is the loving caretaker and sympathetic observer of all Americans:

> Every kind for itself and its own, . . .
> For me those that have been boys and that love women,
> For me the man that is proud and feels how it stings to be slighted,
> For me the sweet-heart and the old maid

and the participant in their lives:

> Of men that live among cattle or taste of the ocean or woods,
> Of the builders and steerers of ships, of the wielders of axes and
> mauls, of the drivers of horses,
> I can eat and sleep with them week in and week out.

He is the self-appointed, supreme teller of their story:

> And I know I am solid and sound,
> To me the converging objects of the universe perpetually flow,
> All are written to me, and I must get what the writing means.

Whitman is the divinely inspired poet, the one who can read the hidden book of nature and reveal its meanings:

> I guess the grass is itself a child . . .
> Or I guess it is a uniform hieroglyphic,
> And it means, Sprouting alike in broad zones and narrow zones,

> Growing among black folks as among white,

Kanuck, Tuckahoe, Congressman, Cuff, I give them the same, I receive them the same.

Indeed, the idea of reading the book of nature is a mystical one, a direct communication with God and, based on this direct communication, Whitman offers the ultimate consolation of reading immortality into all forms of life, assuring us that death is not to be feared but anticipated as a stepping-stone to rebirth:

> The smallest sprout shows there is really no death,
> And if ever there was it led forward life, and does not wait at the
>   end to arrest it,
> And ceased the moment life appeared.
> All goes onward and outward. . . . and nothing collapses,
> And to die is different from what any one supposed, and luckier.

Whitman celebrates the body and makes it coequal with the soul:

> If I worship one thing more than another it shall be the spread of
>   my own body, or any part of it,
> Translucent mould of me it shall be you!

He tells the story that convention considers unfit for poetry, and he tells it in the same language he hears it:

> What living and buried speech is always vibrating here, what howls
>   restrain'd by decorum,
> Arrests of criminals, slights, adulterous offers made . . .
> I mind them or the show or resonance of them.

Despite his self-congratulation and self-aggrandizement, Whitman's charm resides in his love for his people and his desire to include all Americans in a feast of conversation, praise, encouragement, sympathy, and hospitality:

> Stop this day and night with me and you shall possess the origin
>   of all poems.

His love seeks to bind all diversity into a unified oneness, still preserving the integrity of the individual. He goes beyond the immediate world of isolated moments and transforms these moments into a promise of return. In the end, Whitman becomes more than a national poet; he becomes a citizen of the world and all its people, convinced of his own limitless powers, which he bequeaths to all others:

My faith is the greatest of faiths and the least of faiths,
Enclosing all worship ancient and modern, and all between ancient
and modern,
Believing I shall come again upon the earth after five thousand
years. ❀

Critical Views on
"Song of Myself"

[Stephen Tapscott has written several volumes of poetry as well as an essay entitled *American Beauty: William Carlos Williams and the Modernist Whitman*. In the excerpt below, Tapscott discusses images of the body as ideal political structure within the context of specific political facts in "Song of Myself."]

In the genealogy of the "Whitman strain" of American poetry, Whitman is the forebear poet most overtly committed to the "instruction" of his readers for specific historical *and* spiritual formation. I think it important to remember that Whitman published "Song of Myself" in 1855, the year after the Congress effectively repealed the Missouri Compromise of 1820 (which declared that slavery was prohibited in most of the areas in the Louisiana Purchase) by passing the Kansas-Nebraska Act of 1854 (which called for "popular sovereignty" in the new territories and made room for the Supreme Court's Dred Scott decision in 1856). In 1847, the U.S. had taken control of vast territories in the Southwest, including Texas—2/3 of the land-mass of Mexico—during the Mexican War, and the question of the legality of slavery in those territories was also under heated discussion; there was some talk about annexing Cuba, as a slave state, to increase the number of Southern states. The nation was clearly on the path towards Civil War, and—as these few examples suggest—the terms of much of the national discussion involved questions of the autonomy of the physical landscape and the question of the nature of the economic system that would be imposed on newly-acquired territories. I think it is fair—and necessary—to read Whitman's poems as in large part a constructivist argument in favor of new cultural forms in this social context. Whitman is not *only* a "relativist" and Jacksonian patriot and disciple of Emersonian doctrines about the Transcendental Oversoul in its Moment and about the formal self-reliance of the American psyche—though it is possible to read him through those lenses. For Whitman the political and the spiritual commitments of American poetry came together very directly. Especially in his poems before the Civil War, it is difficult to distinguish when Whitman is talking about the ideal political structure he envisions for America, when he is describing the perfect spiritual structure of Democratic Individualism, and when he is talking about his Ideal Representative Self: all three concepts coincide. In Whitman's poems just before the war—significantly, those to which the Modern generations paid the closest attention—we hear the voice of a man calling for unity, a spiritual and political unification grounded in the integrity of the American continent and in the autonomy of his own body; he is generously offering himself as a metaphor for integrity or for integration, hugely projecting an image of his personal synthetic identity as a model for other forms of synthesis, both intellectual and political. [. . .]

He writes in order to define new assimilative, synthetic, cultural forms as models for the processes of self-forgiveness, cultural integration, and political unification (somatic, continent-wide) he considers essential to the nation's future. And yet, at the same time, these attitudes contain clearly, to my ear, an anxiety about the coherence of the political "body," as well as about the coherence of the Self. In her essay . . . Professor Salska elegantly finds traces of this issue—the anxiety about coherence and autonomy—throughout Whitman's work, much earlier than other critics had traditionally recognized it. [. . .]

Consider this section of "Song of Myself" (1855 version):

> If I worship any particular thing it shall be some of the spread of my
>   body;
> Translucent mould of me it shall be you,
> Shaded ledges and rests, firm masculine coulter, it shall be you,
> Whatever goes to the tilth of me it shall be you,
> You my rich blood, your milky stream pale strippings of my life;
> Breast that presses against other breasts it shall be you,
> My brain it shall be your occult convolutions.
> Root of washed sweet-flag, timorous pond-snipe, nest of guarded
>   duplicate eggs, it shall be you,
> Mixed tussled hay of head and beard and brawn, it shall be you,
> Trickling sap of maple, fibre of manly wheat, it shall be you;
> Sun so generous it shall be you,
> Vapors lighting and shading my face it shall be you,
> You sweaty brooks and dews it shall be you,
> Winds whose soft-tickling genitals rub against me it shall be you,

Broad muscular fields, branches of liveoak, loving lounger in my
  winding paths, it shall be you,
Hands I have taken, face I have kissed, mortal I have ever touched, it
  shall be you.
I dote on myself. . . there is that lot of me, and all so luscious,
Each moment and whatever happens thrills me with joy.

Here Whitman is arguing with several purposes—including a specific historical purpose. He wants to describe the integrity of his
physical body in such a way as to suggest the autonomy of the American landscape, independent of the divisive ideological figurations
that might be superimposed on that landscape, and at the same time
to insist on this integrity as a political position. That is Whitman's
purpose, and his political purpose generates his form, that of the list
bound together with an encomium of future praise, "it shall be you";
this is the diction of a *you* mediated by an *it*, the objectified, manifest
and static body of the self-turned-into-landscape.

—Stephen Tapscott, "Whitman in 1855 and the Image of the 'Body
Politic,' in " *Utopia in the Present Tense* (Rome: University of Macerata, 1994): pp. 112–15.

MARK BAUERLEIN ON THE SPEAKING VOICE IN "SONG OF MYSELF"

[Mark Bauerlein is author of *Whitman and the American
Idiom, The Turning Word: American Literary Modernism* and
*Continental Theory and the Pragmatic Mind: Explorations in the
Psychology of Belief.* In the excerpt below, Bauerlein discusses
how Whitman's message in "Song of Myself" is made all the
more powerful by a speaking voice which directly addresses the
audience, rather than a textual presentation of a poem.]

Because writing separates the author both from his own language and
from his audience (who therefore "take things at second or third
hand"), writing precludes an immediate communal experience—
exactly what Whitman wants to inspire in his readers. Writing puts each
reader into his own private study, and so the "truth" of "Song of Myself"
becomes fragmented in solipsistic, idiosyncratic interpretations beyond

the author's control. To preserve and share the experience of "Song of Myself," Whitman must return to a speaker-audience relation, where the "breath of laws and songs and behavior," under the auspices of the governing source of inspiration, can be passed between one another without corruption. Because speech springs up naturally and immediately from experience without prescription or regulation by technics or propriety (which, as conventional, can change through history), speech can make claims to universality. It "encompass[es] volumes of worlds" (and books). It takes place with the fact while writing takes place after the fact, involving a reconstruction of and a separation from presence. Writing refers to a remembered past, speech inhabits a living present. Speech then becomes Whitman's major tactical motif in "Song of Myself" that harmonizes and consolidates society into a unified "interpretive community." [. . .]

The situation of the physicist reading the "Book of Nature" has its analogue in the critic engaged in reading the poem. In the case of "Song of Myself," the critic's "unified field theory" is the author whose coherent, ruling personality stabilizes and elucidates the poem by providing an ultimate referent for its meaning. But instead of a blank, mechanical set of atomic processes to theorize about, the reader of Whitman has a vibrant, congenial "brother" ready to offer interpretive guidance and even demand a sympathetic rejoinder. Whitman's concern to direct the reader's response is evidenced by open addresses scattered throughout the poem from the first section—"And what I assume you shall assume"—to the last—"I stop somewhere waiting for you." But to assert his continued though benevolent authority over the reader, Whitman must inject his speaking presence into the poem, and so the problem becomes one of how to bypass the fallen, distancing written signifier, how to convince the reader that "this is no book;/ Who touches this, touches a man."

The idea that the book can become a coextension of Whitman's physical body which the reader can luxuriate in neatly accords with [John T.] Irwin's thesis. He extends his hieroglyphic interpretation of "Song of Myself" by claiming that Whitman's desire for contact with the reader goes further than the avowal of presence in the form of speech. Whitman intends to use an even more immediate, self-evident signification with which to gather in his readers in the mutual celebration not only of sonic but also of tactile experience.

The kind of immediately convincing presence that Whitman has in mind is not the presence of a speaking voice but of a physical body.... Whitman's poems are intended to be outlines of the body —hieroglyphic gestures. (Irwin, *American Hieroglyphics*, p. 98)

With the transferral of preferred signs from the oral/aural to the physiognomic/pictographic, Whitman discovers the most impressive means of communication he can find: "Writing and talk do not prove me,/ I carry the plenum of proof and every thing else in my face." Not in what his face expresses in any linguistic sense, not in any idea which causes a facial expression (the latter then being a mediation, a facade, for an anterior and non-spatial motive), but in his countenance itself. Just as the mute face of nature peremptorily interrupts Whitman's frivolity—"the look of the bay mare shames silliness out of me"—so Whitman's patient dumbness thwarts those who would mock him— "With the hush of my lips I wholly confound the skeptic." A mystical silence overrules language.

But, of course, Whitman does use language and he does so in a notation that is never pictographic. So how does Whitman convey his personal physiognomy to the reader other than proclaiming his silence (an oxymoron), by printing a picture of himself on the title page with no signature (a genuinely pictographic sign but one which is nevertheless incomplete until the figure is named in Section 24), and by repeated sensualistic allusions to his corporeal body (references mediated nonetheless by an arbitrary, abstract, bodiless sign system). Irwin offers a concise yet far-reaching explanation of how Whitman's poetic strategy transmits the visible poetic self to the reader and renders mediation harmless.

—Mark Bauerlein, "The Written Orator of 'Song of Myself,'" *Walt Whitman Quarterly Review* 3, no. 3 (Winter 1986): pp. 2, 4–5.

BETSY ERKKILA ON NINETEENTH-CENTURY POLITICS IN "SONG OF MYSELF"

[Betsy Erkkila has written extensively on Whitman and is the author of *Walt Whitman Among the French: Poet and*

Myth and *Whitman the Political Poet*. In the excerpt from her article, Erkkila situates "Song of Myself" in the republican ideals of early nineteenth-century artisan radicalism, balancing independence and community, personal wealth and commonwealth.]

This vision of a poet stretching within a universe bounded by pride and sympathy had as its political analogue the paradox of an American republic poised between self-interest and public virtue, liberty and union, the interests of the many and the good of the one. The secret not only of Whitman's art but of the American Union, the paradox of many in one, would eventually become the opening inscription and balancing frame of *Leaves of Grass*:

> One's-Self I sing, a simple separate person,
> Yet utter the word Democratic, the word En-Masse.

Balanced between the separate person and the people en masse, the politics of *Leaves of Grass* is neither liberal nor bourgeois in the classical sense of either term; rather, the poems inscribe the republican ideals of early nineteenth-century artisan radicalism, emphasizing the interlinked values of independence and community, of personal wealth and commonwealth.

Whitman's concern with the problem of individual power, balance, and social union was in part a response to the political turmoil of the 1840s and 1850s—a time when traditional republican values were being eroded as America was transformed from an agrarian to an industrial economy and the political Union was itself dissolving under the pressure of the contradiction of slavery in the American republic. In this essay, I discuss ways to read and teach "Song of Myself" as a poem that grows out of, and responds to, revolutionary ideology and the specific political struggles of America on the eve of the Civil War.

Just as the American Revolution had led to a relocation of authority inside rather than outside the individual, so Whitman's myth of origins focused not on the exploits of a historic or mythic figure of the past but on the heroism of a self who was, like the nation, in the process of creation. Whitman mythologizes what he called the "entire faith and acceptance" (*Prose Works* 2: 729) of the American republic in a poetic person who is at once a model of democratic character and a figure of democratic union. Speaking of the analogy between the individual and the body politic, he said:

"What is any Nation—after all—and what is a human being—but a struggle between conflicting, paradoxical, opposing elements—and they themselves and the most violent contests, important parts of that One Identity, and of its development?" (*Whitman's Memoranda* 65).

The drama of identity in "Song of Myself" is rooted in the political drama of a nation in crisis—a nation, as Lincoln observed at the time, living in the midst of alarms and anxiety in which "we expect some new disaster with each newspaper we read" (Sandburg vii). Through the invention of an organic self who is like the Union, many in one, Whitman seeks to balance and reconcile major conflicts in the American body politic: the conflicts between "separate person" and "en masse," individualism and equality, liberty and union, the South and the North, the farm and the city, labor and capital, black and white, female and male, and religion and science. In teaching "Song of Myself," one might discuss the ways these conflicts are played out in individual sections. [. . .]

Like the American republic, "Song of Myself" is an experiment in self-governance that both tests and illustrates the capacity of a muscular and self-possessed individual for regulation from within. The poem might be read as a democratic performance in which the poet approaches the limit of sexual appetite and hellish despair but is continually restored to an inward economy of equity and balance. In his famous act of self-naming in section 24, Whitman stresses his sexually turbulent nature:

> Walt Whitman, a kosmos, of Manhattan the son,
> Turbulent, fleshy, sensual, eating, drinking and breeding,
> No sentimentalist, no stander above men and women or apart from
>   them,
> No more modest than immodest.
> Unscrew the locks from the doors!
> Unscrew the doors themselves from their jambs! (*LG* 52)

Here as throughout the poem Whitman celebrates and indeed flaunts his representative status as a poet who absorbs into the "kosmos" of his body and his poem what he called in his journalism the "turbulence and destructiveness" and "freaks and excesses" of the democratic spirit (*Gathering* 1: 3–4).

It is on the sexual plane, through a release of libidinous energies, that Whitman's democratic poet undergoes his first major trial of self-mastery. The main challenge comes with the onslaught of touch in section 28. The passage records a crisis in which Whitman's hitherto balanced persona, stimulated by a masturbatory fantasy, is taken over by the sense of touch:

> Is this then a touch? quivering me to a new identity,
> Flames and ether making a rush for my veins,
> Treacherous tip of me reaching and crowding to help them,
> My flesh and blood playing out lightning to strike what is hardly different from myself,
> On all sides prurient provokers stiffening my limbs,
> Straining the udder of my heart for its withheld drip. (*LG* 57)

—Betsy Erkkila, "'Song of Myself' and the Politics of the Body Erotic," in *Approaches to Teaching Whitman's Leaves of Grass* (New York: Modern Language Association of America, 1990): pp. 56–58.

Michael D. Reed on Cataloging and the First Person in "Song of Myself"

[In this excerpt, Michael D. Reed discusses how the use of two rhetorical devices, cataloging and the first person "I," are combined to form a difficult yet skillfully balanced definition of nineteenth-century American democracy.]

Originally published in 1855, Whitman's 'Song of Myself,' untitled at first publication, is one of the central poetic achievements of the Transcendental movement that characterized and gave energy to the Renaissance of American Literature during the 19th century. Though Whitman was not himself a Transcendental minister or philosopher, his poetry was instantly recognized by Emerson as a poetic expression of the basic ideas contained in his own essays and lectures. [...]

Whitman combined in his poem two rhetorical devices used extensively by Emerson and the other Transcendentalists, Thoreau, Alcott and Parkinson, that is, the catalogue and the first person persona. Perhaps, more than any other rhetorical elements, these two devices distinguish American Transcendental writings from those of other eras and countries. [...]

Whitman was, of course, the self-proclaimed poet of democracy and the conjunction of these two rhetorical devices in 'Song of Myself' raises an interesting question, for the catalogue, as a great leveling device, would appear to stand in contradiction to the extreme individualism expressed by the first person persona in the poem. In other words, what is the relationship between these two rhetorical devices, and how can they be contained within the same poem? Since Whitman was the poet of democracy, any answer to this question must properly begin with an understanding of how the conjunction of these two rhetorical devices serves as an expression of Whitman's theory of democracy. [...]

America's experiment with democracy in the 19th century was a unique political experiment, and it prompted examination and commentary from foreign and American observers alike. For Whitman, democracy was a fascinating and central theme that occupied his prose and gave life and meaning to his poetry. Democracy, as he understood and explained it, contained two opposed elements: the individual and the aggregate. Whitman, Like Emerson and the other Transcendentalists, laid great stress on the individual element, on individual freedom and expression. [...]

But, Whitman, and the other Transcendentalists, were acutely aware of the paradox created at the very heart of this theory of democracy, for, as they explained America's political system, it contained equally the idea of a strong individualism and the democratic whole. These two elements created a contradiction, for all men could not be equal and individualistic at the same time. [...]

Throughout the catalogues there is a dual purpose; to display diversity and to create unity from the diversity. To create the sense of diversity, Whitman individualizes each item of the catalogue usually with one or two words which describe the action of the subject. For example, consider these items from the catalogue in Section 15:

> The duck-shooter walks by silent and cautious stretches ...
> The youth lies awake in the cedar-roof'd garret and harks to the musical rain ...
> The drover watching his drove sings out to them that would stray.

In each of these lines, and in many more, Whitman expresses the essence of the individual. The 'silent and cautious stretches' of the 'duck-shooter' captures the anticipation and excitement of hunting water fowl along cat-tail lined streams. The 'musical rain' portrays the essence of listening to rain on the roof when we were young, perhaps resting in the afternoon and dreaming. The protective care of the drover is characterized in his concern for each animal 'that would stray.' Thus, in each case, Whitman individualizes the subjects of the lines. He gives us the essence of 'The connoisseur,' 'The Missourian,' and 'The opium-eater,' individualizing each without falling prone to stereotypical figures. Then, through the poetic devices of the catalogues, he brings all the individuals into a poetic whole which becomes a symbol for the democratic 'En-Masse.'

Because of the enormous variety of subjects, the catalogues in 'Song of Myself' appear essentially unstructured, almost disorganized. Yet those multitudinous lists of items are joined together by such poetic devices as consonance, assonance, alliteration, grammatical parallelism and initial rhyme, as we see in the following lines from the expansive catalogue in Section 33 of 'Song of Myself.'

> Where the heifers browse, where geese nip their food with short
> jerks,
> Where sun-down shadows lengthen over the limitless and lonesome
> prairie,
> Where herds of buffalo make a crawling spread of the square miles
> far and near,
> Where the humming-bird shimmers, where the neck of the
> long-lived swan is curing and winding.[...]

Thus, through language and his poetic devices, Whitman can create an actual whole from the diversity of America. The language, the words themselves, becomes a living reality. And this applies equally to the 'I' of 'Song of Myself,' to the first person persona. Hence, by creating a reality through his language and the piling up of images in his catalogues, Whitman is creating himself, the 'I' of the poem. In this way, he creates simultaneously the 'En-Masse' and the strong individual:

> And these tend inward to me, and I tend outward to them,
> And such as it is to be these more or less I am.
> And of these one and all I weave the song of myself.

—Michael D. Reed, "First Person Persona and the Catalogue in 'Song of Myself,'" *Walt Whitman Review* 23, no. 4 (December 1977): pp. 147–51.

Thematic Analysis of
"I Sing the Body Electric"

"I Sing the Body Electric," simply entitled Poem No. 1 in the original 1855 edition of *Leaves of Grass,* acquired its permanent title in the 1867 edition. It is a poem celebrating the body as an essential, indivisible, and inextricable component of the soul. "And if the body does not do fully as much as the soul?/ And if the body were not the soul, what is the soul?" and the effort expended on the part of the poet throughout this poem is the breaking down and removing of all mental and language barriers that inhibit this connection. Much of Whitman's strategy is contained in his use of the word "balk," a word that means both an obstacle (here, a point of view that insists on maintaining the division between body and soul) and the confronting of that obstacle through argument. "The love of the body of man or woman balks account, the body/ itself balks account," a statement that both celebrates human sexuality and asserts that the body does not comprise the total identity of man—it must include his soul.

In later versions of the poem, "I Sing the Body Electric" was divided into nine sections. Section 1 begins with the poet drawing the battle lines, placing himself in the middle of the melee:

> I sing the body electric,
> The armies of those I love . . .
> They will not let me off till I go with them, respond to them,
> And discorrupt and charge them full with the charge of the soul.

Whitman's use of bellicose, hostile imagery introduces us to the feverish intensity of emotions that will soon become evident during the course of his argument. Section 1 sets forth Whitman's agenda in the poem: to respond to and overturn a long historical and literary tradition in which the body is morally antagonistic to the soul. He does this by asking from the outset, "Was it doubted that those who corrupt their own bodies conceal themselves?" thus blaming those who fear and deny their bodies of the same corruption they vigorously try to avoid. Whitman's use of the word "corruption" indicates the sense of incompleteness that results from denying the body's sexuality: "And if those who defile the living are as bad as they who defile the dead?"

In section 2, Whitman advocates joyous participation in the sensual life as a cure for the moral destruction that results from the rejection of that sensuality:

> The expression of a well-made man appears not only in his face,
> It is in his limbs and joints . . .
> To see him pass conveys as much as the best poem, perhaps more.

The poem rebels against many of the beliefs on which the American nation was founded, namely the Puritan tradition and its severe restrictions on sexuality. Thus, "I Sing the Body Electric" represents the soul of America, embodying all of man and nature, with the poet himself as the self-appointed healer. Indeed, Whitman is advocating a new separation, not between body and soul, but instead from all those creeds that deny the full integration of all aspects of human existence. Section 2 continues this song of celebration, the poet taking in all ages and groups, male and female, from all walks of life and occupations, within his loving embrace:

> The sprawl and fulness of babes, the bosoms and heads of women
> . . .
> The swimmer naked in the swimming bath, . . .
> Girls, mothers, house-keepers, in all their performances . . .
> The wrestle of wrestlers . . .
> The natural, perfect, varied attitudes.

Section 3 diverts from the poet's original argument. It is the story of a common farmer, described in meticulous and flattering physical detail, "of wonderful vigor, calmness, beauty of person," who is loved by his children for who he is and not by "allowance." We are thus free to love this man or any other we may choose, "to sit by him in the boat that you and he might touch each other." Indeed, the poet tells us that genuine love comes about not through fear or obligation, but through the freedom to think and choose for ourselves. And, as we are told in section 4, to love whomever we choose is a complete and rewarding freedom because it is a love of both body and soul:

> I have perceiv'd that to be with those I like is enough,
> To stop in company with the rest at evening is enough,
> To be surrounded by beautiful, curious, breathing, laughing flesh
> is enough.

Section 5 returns to the theme in the title, "the body electric," and the poet's self-appointed role as liberator and animator of this newly integrated body. Whitman creates a democracy of full participation and equality of the sexes; he addresses the female body directly, eschewing the belief in the superiority of men over women, and revels in the attractiveness of its form and its powerful magnetism:

> This is the female form,
> A divine nimbus exhales from it head to foot.
> It attracts with fierce undeniable attraction.

Whitman overturns the Judeo-Christian belief that, as Eve was the cause of Adam's fall, so all women are the source of corruption in the world:

> Books, art, religion, time, the visible and solid earth . . . the atmosphere and the fringed clouds . . . what was expected of heaven or fear'd of hell, are now consumed.

The female body is worshiped as the precise site for entering the soul:

> Be not ashamed women . . . your privilege encloses the rest . . . it is the exit of the rest,
> You are the gates of the body and you are the gates of the soul.

Whitman thus rejects all systems of belief that contradict the integrity of the body and employ instead the threat of eternal damnation as a means of control.

Section 6 continues the theme of equality between the sexes—a radical notion in 1850s America—this time celebrating the role of the male as part of the divine purpose of the universe: "The male is not less the soul nor more, he too is in his place,/ He too is all qualities. . . . he is action and power" and his body is equally as sacred as the woman's.

Sections 7 and 8 consider the male and female bodies of slaves being sold at auction and the rupture in the social fabric that goes even beyond the individual being denied his birthright:

> This is not only one man, this the father of those who shall be fathers in their turns,
> In him the start of populous states and rich republics,
> Of him countless immortal lives with countless embodiments and enjoyments.

Likewise, the woman, "too is not only herself, she is the teeming mother of mothers."

Section 9, the conclusion of the poem, is a summing up in meticulous anatomical detail of the newly integrated man whom the poet has lovingly reconstructed:

> All attitudes, all the shapeliness, all the belongings of my or your
>   body or any one's body, male or female.
> The healthy man represents a spiritually redeemed society:
> The exquisite realization of health, . . .
> These are not the parts and poems of the body only, but of the soul.

This newly revitalized body becomes a part of the natural landscape, "the circling rivers the breath, and breathing it in and out." In the end, Whitman has broken down the barriers that stand in the way of true equality by collapsing a poetic tradition that struggled and resisted against the yoking of the body to the soul. ❁

Critical Views on
"I Sing the Body Electric"

HAROLD ASPIZ ON SCIENCE AND SEX IN
"I SING THE BODY ELECTRIC"

[Harold Aspiz is a well-known Whitman scholar and the author of *Walt Whitman and the Body Beautiful*. In the excerpt below, Aspiz discusses the concept of a body electricity in terms of Whitman's persona as a vitalizing life force and as a contemporary scientific issue influencing his poetry in several ways.]

The phrase 'the body electric' appears only twice in *Leaves of Grass*, but the recurrent concept of a body electric serves to define the Whitman persona's vitalizing life force, his astonishing masculinity, his cosmic selfhood, and his mystic transcendence of life and death. It is understandable that Whitman should have been inspired by the infinitely hopeful science of electricity, for when *Leaves of Grass* first appeared investigations into the physical and chemical nature of electricity and its manifestations in man had been undertaken by many distinguished experimenters; 'electrical' ideas had infiltrated the writings of Alcott, Poe, and Melville; and the belief that electricity might one day reveal the secrets of life had fired the popular imagination. Of course, Whitman (like most nonscientific intellectuals of his time) made no careful distinctions in the extensive spectrum of electrical lore which ranged from scientifically verifiable fact to theories of electro-spiritualism.

The electrical concepts in *Leaves of Grass* can be roughly paralleled in works that Whitman is known to have read. Thus, a volume on mesmerism that he perused a dozen years before composing *Leaves of Grass* defined the body as 'an electrical machine' and stated: 'Facts prove that our bodies are electric and that the degree of electricity varies in different individuals.' Acting on the principle that the more electricity one possesses the better, the Whitman persona boasts of his electric 'stores plenty and to spare' and in several passages of *Leaves of Grass*, appears to be an inexhaustible electric generator.

A book by a Fowlers and Wells author, which the poet read, described electricity as the 'subtle fluid [which] seems to form the connecting link between the soul and the body, and to be the instrument by means of which the former builds, rebuilds, or shapes the latter. It is generally supposed to be electric or magnetic in its nature. The ancient Magians called it the living fire.' (The familiar concept that electricity is a fire or a rarefied fluid is echoed in Whitman's poetic references to the 'subtle fluid' and 'the subtle electric fire.') In a similar vein, America's outstanding phrenologist Orson S. Fowler explained that magnetism, or electricity, or galvanism . . . is now conceded to be the grand agent or instrumentality of life in all its forms. . . .' And another called electricity 'the universal agent by which man rules over matter, whether the mind be finite or infinite.' Thus we may reasonably assume that the electric component of the body electric is literally *electric*.

Many of the poems in *Leaves of Grass* depict the persona as an electro-magnetic superman whose body attracts 'all I meet or know.' His sexuality is electrical. The sexual forces 'that draw me [Whitman-Adam] so close by tender directions and indirections' are magnetic. To the lover who sits beside him, he tells 'of the subtle electric fire that for your sake is playing within me.' With electrical bravado, he declares:

> Know, I am a man, attracting, at any time, her I but look upon, or
> touch with the tips of my fingers,
> Or that touches my face, or leans against me.

[. . .] A book presented to Whitman by a scientist friend argued that sick persons are benefited by the direct application of electricity and documented the efficacy of the electric battery in alleviating or curing a broad range of mental and physical ailments. Roughly analogous claims were made by mesmerists and faith healers for the effusions of personal electricity in healing the sick and distressed. [. . .]

The persona, too, appears to be a magnetic healer who transfers his electric surplusage to the sufferers' nervous systems and thus stimulates their vital electrical powers. In trial lines for 'Song of Myself,' the persona infuses a weak comrade with 'grit and jets of life' in order to cure him. And in Sections 39, 40, and 41 of 'Song of Myself' electric 'emanations' issue from the persona's glance and the tips of his fingers and are 'wafted with the odor of my body or breath.' [. . .]

The persona's capacity for ideal fatherhood is also stated in electrical terms. An English spiritualist physician, in a book that the poet read, described the life-giving element in the human blood as electric. Like Whitman, the doctor assumed that the open air contains the electricity by which the blood is oxygenated and vitalized—a concept (articulated by reputable scientists) which the poet elaborated in describing the physically and spiritually regenerative properties of the air/afflatus in 'Song of the Open Road.' And the English physician also implied that the *sperm* is an electric nucleus—*the sole source and transmitter of human and animal life*—a concept fundamental to the understanding of Whitman's 'body electric.'

—Harold Aspiz, "'The Body Electric': Science, Sex, and Metaphor," *Walt Whitman Review* 24, no. 4 (December 1978): pp. 137–139.

M. JIMMIE KILLINGSWORTH ON CONTEMPORARY MEDICAL SCIENCE IN "I SING THE BODY ELECTRIC"

[M. Jimmie Killingsworth is the author of *Whitman's Poetry of the Body: Sexuality, Politics and the Text.* In this excerpt, Killingsworth discusses the poem "I Sing the Body Electric" in terms of Whitman's reading of contemporary medical science.]

In 1856 Whitman added to his 'Poem of the Body,' as it was then titled, a new first line—'I sing the body electric.' In this poem, if not in many of those cited by Ms. Sulfrudge, the sense of 'electric' depends upon connotations not readily discernible to modern readers. It is my contention that Whitman drew the word from the vocabulary of contemporary medical science rather than from physics or technology. Moreover, in 'I Sing the Body Electric,' he borrowed the concept of 'sexual electricity' from the medical writers of sex education literature, thereby infusing the poem with language and ideas apparent in most reputable discussions of sex in the 1850s and 1860s.

As the poet of the body in the 1855, 1857 and 1860 editions of the *Leaves,* Whitman's interest in human sexuality and its expression in art led him to seek trustworthy, scientific instruction on the subject. In a personal note of the 1850s, he reminds himself to 'Read the latest and best anatomical works. Talk with physicians.' Apparently the poet was sincere in this intention, for among the scrapbooks of Whitman's papers in the Library of Congress there are numerous clippings from works like *Hall's Journal of Health*, the *Water-Cure Journal*, and the *American Phrenological Journal*, writings considered by many contemporaries to be 'the latest and best anatomical works.' Whitman's preoccupation with health is self-evident, and in 'Song of Myself' he affirms his credentials as well as his faith in physicality:

> Having pried through the strata, analyzed to a hair, counsel'd with doctors and calculated close,
> I find no sweeter fat than sticks to my own bones.

The theory of sexual electricity was popular among the medical writers with whom Whitman was surely familiar. Implications of the concept appear as early as 1849, though it seems that the theory was not refined until the middle 1850s and early 1860s. The fullest and clearest statement of the electrical qualities of sexuality appears in Dr. Edward H. Dixon's 1861 pamphlet *The Organic Law of the Sexes: Positive and Negative Electricity and the Abnormal Conditions that Impair Vitality*, which summarizes ideas previously advanced by Dr. Dixon and other educators. It is reasonable to assume that Whitman knew of these precepts during the time he was publishing the second edition of *Leaves of Grass* with Fowler and Wells in 1856. His knowledge of Dixon's thought and works is evidenced by his review of the doctor's book *Woman and Her diseases, from the Cradle to the Grave*. [...]

Furthermore, in his notebook toward the 1856 edition of *Leaves of Grass*, Whitman has noted the name and address of the editor of the popular medical magazine, *The Scalpel*, namely, Edward H. Dixon, 42 Fifth Avenue.

Dixon's presentation of the 'organic law of the sexes' will of course seem rather ridiculous in light of present-day scientific knowledge, but during the middle years of the 19th century little was known of electricity's true nature. Thus all sorts of bizarre powers were assigned to that force, as well as to magnetism and related manifestations. [...]

Man can never be whole until he experiences and gives in to the sexual power of the mother-woman: 'after the child is born of woman....' Therefore, sex is the agent through which man realizes 'the forcefulness or power of the quintessential life experience,' to use Cynthia Sulfrudge's terms. [...]

Regardless of the particular source, it is clear from his use of language and ideas in 'I Sing the Body Electric' that Whitman was aware of the theory which held sex to be an electrobiological function through which man is able to find his 'place in the grand cosmogony.' Like Dixon and Fowler, the 'lusty and liberal' poet of the early *Leaves of Grass* understood sex as a human manifestation of the universal tendency of things to attract and become whole.

—M. Jimmie Killingsworth, "Another Source for Whitman's Use of 'Electric,'" *Walt Whitman Review* 23, no. 3 (September 1977): pp. 129–132.

ROBERT COSKREN ON THE BODY IN MOVEMENT IN "I SING THE BODY ELECTRIC"

[In the excerpt below, Robert Coskren, a professor at Pennsylvania State University, discusses the parable of Section 3 of the poem as a gathering together of various aspects of the body in movement, finding virtue in Whitman's ability (unlike prior critics) to combine flesh, spirit, and universe, which pervades all of *Leaves of Grass*.]

Walt Whitman's poem, 'I Sing the Body Electric,' has had an unfortunate critical history. Emerson, for instance, recommended that Whitman withdraw this poem from the 'Children of Adam' group because of its apparent unseemliness. D. H. Lawrence, on the other hand, attacked the poem on artistic grounds, calling its final catalog a 'horrible pottage of human parts.' A modern critic, Richard Chase, complained of the poem in terms of the weakness of its conception and argued that 'Whitman's celebration of the body and of procreation are fatally lacking in emotion.' Whatever truth there is in such accusations—and that this poem is not one of Whitman's finest can hardly be denied—it is equally true that this poem represents the poet's first extensive attempt to apprehend in poetry that peculiar combination of drives, flesh and spirit which is the human body. This poem provides, therefore, Whitman's own commentary on what is surely a central image in the vast bulk of his poetry.

Examining 'I Sing the Body Electric,' we discover that Whitman conceives the human body, finally, in the broadest possible terms; that is, as that particular organization of flesh and blood which participates in the elemental forces of the universe. The 'body electric' is the human body in movement, in a motion paralleling the recurrent motion of the universe itself. The 'body electric' is the literal movement of the body; it is also the instinctive movement of one body toward another. The 'body electric' resolves the soul within the body, the soul being the perfect and vital equilibrium of the parts of the body.

Section 1 introduces the argument of the poem as a series of questions and cryptic assertions. On one hand, Whitman explicitly assumes the age-old question of the relation of the body to the soul [. . .] In addition, Whitman intends to explore the difference between the corrupt and healthy body. He exclaims,

> I sing the body electric,
> The armies of those I love engirth me and I engirth them,
> They will not let me off till I go with them, respond to them,
> And discorrupt them, and charge them full with the charge of the soul.

These lines raise still further questions: what is the nature of the soul? What is this force which 'discorrupts'? Of what does the 'body electric' consist? And of what does the 'charge of the soul' consist? Whitman's answer to these questions is implicit in his insistence upon the quality of movement in the vital soul. [. . .]

Section 2 furthers the poet's exploration of the body in movement. And, in fact, as if to forestall any apprehension of the body in merely rational or conceptual terms—in some category, that is, outside of the body itself—Whitman hints,

> The love of the body of man or woman balks account, the body itself balks account . . .
> The expression of the face balks account.

Here the poet asserts the essential mystery of the human body: it is unaccountable. On the other hand, Whitman sees in the moving, active body the unanticipated expression of itself; for, while the body 'balks account,' the expression of the 'well-made man' appears 'in his walk'; it is in 'the carriage of his neck', it is in 'the flex of his waist.' In movement, therefore, the body expresses itself. [...]

Sections 3 and 4 insist upon the mysterious attractiveness of the active body. In Section 3 Whitman offers what might be termed a parable of the body electric. He envisions a man whose chief quality is his 'vigor' (mentioned twice) and activity—'He was a frequent gunner and fisher'—and of his consequent attractiveness to those about him. Whitman notes,

> They and his daughters loved him, all who saw him loved him,
> They did not love him by allowance, they loved him with personal love.

The quality of love which this man inspires is not artificial, not, perhaps, rational, but a complete and mutual attraction. It represents a movement of the body as well as the soul, as Whitman makes explicit in the final lines of the stanza:

> You would wish long to be with him, you would wish to sit by him in the boat that you and he might touch each other.

Section 3, then, begins to gather together the various qualities of the body in movement within a pattern. In this parable, for instance, Whitman introduces a man who is loved. The love represents a response of the beholder to his vigorous, active body. Thus, the literal movement of a body inspires a spiritual movement (a response) in others. And the spiritual movement, the attraction of love, results in a charged response to the body ('that you and he might touch each other'). Whitman has begun to weave his images into a pattern; in doing so he begins to treat of the relation of the body to the soul. Implicit in this 'parable,' for instance, is the key to Whitman's treatment of the apparent dichotomy: in movement the body and soul meet in equilibrium....

The poem concludes with a final affirmation of the essential indissolubility of the body and soul. Having completed, for instance, the catalog in images suggestive of the body in movement, of the body 'leaping' and 'reclining' and 'embracing' or 'curving,' of the body 'tightening' and 'circling' or 'breathing,' and having gathered these images together in a central image suggestive of the perfect equilibrium of its (the body's) moving parts—'The exquisite realization of health'—Whitman is able to assert finally,

> O I say these are not the parts and poems of the body only, but of the soul,
> O I say now these are the soul!

—Robert Coskren, "A Reading of Whitman's 'I Sing the Body Electric,'" *Walt Whitman Review* 22, no. 3 (September 1976): pp. 125–28, 131–32.

Thematic Analysis of
"The Sleepers"

Originally untitled in the 1855 edition of *Leaves of Grass,* then titled "Night Poem" in 1856, then "Sleep Chasings" in 1860, it was called finally "The Sleepers" in 1871. Highly imaginative, it has been described as one of Whitman's most problematic poems. "The Sleepers" has received a range of critical perspectives: It has been described, variously, as a poem about the making of the poet and the growth of his own imagination; a setting forth of the poet's doctrine of rebirth and return after death; a landscape of the unconscious mind during a dream state; a confessional about the poet's child-hood and his growth into manhood and adult sexuality; and a vision of a psychic journey in which the poet begins in confusion and ends in a state of pure harmony.

In section 1, the poet wanders aimlessly, lost to himself in his pre-occupation with others:

> I wander all night in my vision,
> Stepping with light feet. . . . swiftly and noiselessly stepping and stopping,
> Bending with open eyes over the shut eyes of sleepers;
> Wandering and confused. . . . lost to myself. . . . ill-assorte . . . . con-tradictory.

The nighttime landscape of section 1 is dark and foreboding, with breathless spirits rushing around. "Breathless" is an apt word for this dreamlike world, describing both the deathlike state of its inhabi-tants and the exhausted energy of the poet/sleepwalker:

> I see nimble ghosts whichever way I look,
> Cache and cache again deep in the ground and sea, and where it is neither ground or sea.

Here is a landscape with unclear boundaries, a world in which one can easily lose one's way. The poet encounters images of other sleepers who are nearly dead themselves, dead of their spiritual and psychological status:

> The wretched features of ennuyes, the white features of corpses, the livid faces of drunkards, the sick-gray faces of onanists,

The gashed bodies on battlefields, the insane in their strong-doored rooms, the sacred idiots,
The newborn emerging from gates and the dying emerging from gates,
The night pervades them and enfolds them.

Whitman is the observer who heals all the suffering around him:

I go from bedside to bedside. . . . I sleep close with the other sleepers, each in turn;
I dream in my dream all the dreams of the other dreamers,
And I become the other dreamers.

Whitman is the spiritual presence that sees what is imperceptible to others and binds all souls together:

Only from me can they hide nothing and would not if they could;
I reckon I am their boss and they make me a pet besides.

Whitman is not only observer, but a full, even outrageous, participant in the care of these restless souls.

As section 1 ends, this nightworld is transformed from threatening to soothing: "Darkness you are gentler than my lover." The poet becomes a participant in the "gay gang of blackguards with mirth-shouting music and wildflapping pennants of joy." Whitman's identification with all other dreamers creates a new sense of wholeness for himself:

I am the actor and the actress . . . the voter . . . the politician,
The emigrant and the exile . . . the criminal that stood in the box,
He who has been famous, and he who shall be famous after today.

In section 2, Whitman removes the suffering of old age by taking on its debilitating effects:

It is my face yellow and wrinkled instead of the old woman's,
I sit low in a strawbottom chair and carefully darn my grandson's stockings.

And then Whitman becomes death itself:

A shroud I see and I am the shroud, I wrap a body and lie in the coffin.
It is dark here underground. . . . it is not evil or pain here. . . . it is blank here, for reasons.

In section 3, Whitman watches a beautiful swimmer:

> I see his white body, I see his undaunted eyes,
> I hate the swift-running eddies that would dash him headforemost
>   on the rocks.

The element of sexual terror, which often accompanies the fear of reaching sexual maturity, is undeniable here in a frighteningly animated landscape:

> Steady and long he struggles;
> He is baffled and banged and bruised. . . . he holds out while his
>   strength holds out,
> The slapping eddies are spotted with his blood. . . . they bear him
>   away. . . . they roll him and swing him and turn him:
> His beautiful body is borne in the circling eddies. . . . it is continually
>   bruised on rocks,
> Swiftly and out of sight is borne the brave corpse.

Destruction recurs in section 4, as the poet is left perplexed in a landscape that has grown dark once more:

> I turn but do not extricate myself;
> Confused. . . . a pastreading. . . . another, but with darkness yet.

The poet here is plaintive, pathetic ("I cannot aid with my wringing fingers"); he gathers up the dead bodies, placing them "in rows in a barn." This battlefield imagery leads to a meditation on war in section 5, as the poet imagines scenes of the American Revolution:

> Washington stands inside the lines . . . he stands on the entrenched
>   hills amid a crowd of officers,
> His face is cold and damp. . . . he cannot repress the weeping drops.

Section 6 continues the poet's meditation, here in a recollection of his dead mother and the story she told him of the Indian squaw who vanished from her life.

Section 7 begins in optimism, conveyed in a series of images that appear in a redemptive nighttime:

> Elements merge in the night. . . . ships make tacks in the dreams. . . .
>   the sailor sails. . . . the exile returns home,
> The fugitive returns unharmed.

Whitman's vision here is idyllic and healing, where

> The consumptive, the erysipalite, the idiot, he that is wronged
> The antipodes, and every one between this and them in the dark

> I swear they are averaged now. . . . one is no better than the other,
> The night and sleep have likened them and restored them.

Section 8 continues with Whitman reviving the sick:

> The swelled and convulsed and congested awake to themselves in
> condition,
> They pass the invigoration of the night and the chemistry of the
> night and awake

and validating the oppressed:

> The call of the slave is one with the master's call,

and ends with the creation of a true and perfect democratic society of dreamers, in which all are equal and the poet reigns supreme:

> I know not how I came of you, and I know not where I go with you,
> . . . . but I know I came well and shall go well. ❀

Critical Views on
"The Sleepers"

CAROL Z. WHELAN ON DEATH AND DISORDER
IN "THE SLEEPERS"

[In the excerpt below, Carol Z. Whelan discusses the death
and disorder of the earlier sections and the final life-
affirming sections of the poem in a psychoanalytic context
that sees the poem as a therapeutic process leading to a
feeling of well-being.]

Walt Whitman's "The Sleepers," "the most famous dream in American literature," a vision where pain, death, and isolation "awaken" to
peace, life, and unity, has produced a variety of readings which
ignore the poem as a process or progression of contraries. Critics
find that Whitman's imagery of death, pain, departure, and disorder
throughout the first six sections of "The Sleepers," is at odds with the
life-affirming "contrastive schema" or "elaborate counterpointing" of
the poem's "contrived" concluding sections. "Whitman's leap of faith
at the end has caused problems," acknowledges one critic. However,
when we read "The Sleepers" as a progression of contraries and
examine its contradictions, we will find that the conclusion of the
poem emphasizes what the poet has been saying since the beginning
of his vision.

To follow Whitman through his dream of "sleep chasings," Julia
Kristeva's eclectic critical approach is helpful: her psychoanalytic
definitions and emphasis on the interdependence of opposites fit a
reading where "The Sleepers" leads us not, as Kerry Larson claims,
"through a grief-stricken maze," but rather through Whitman's
"revolving cycles in their wide sweep" that make up the movements
of life.

"The Sleepers" progresses through a flexible pattern of opposites.
Whitman's familiar "I" oscillates between I-as-witness and I-as-
Other through visions that move from I-as-singular to I-as-plural,
young female to old widow, anonymous giant to historical giant,
father to mother, night to day. If we include the poem's two deleted
sections the pattern is not disrupted: a young male's voice follows
the young female's voice; later a black slave's section follows the

vision of a red squaw (contrasting gender, color and social state). This pattern suggests that under Whitman's apparent disorder sleeps an organic coherence.

The "I" that begins the poem's first four sections with its movements—"I wander," "I descend," "I see," "I turn"—opens the poem with what has been read as a purely negative declaration:

> I wander all night in my vision,
> Stepping with light feet, swiftly and noiselessly stepping and stop-
> ping,
> Bending with open eyes over the shut eyes of sleepers,
> Wandering and confused, lost to myself, ill-assorted, contradictory,
> Pausing, gazing, bending, and stopping.

R. W. French interprets this wandering as pure impotence: "'The Sleepers' begins with the poet as mere dreamer, caught up in his own confusion, powerless, unable to act or to respond sympathetically to the world around him." However, the speaker is *literally* "ill-assorted," invested with opposing elements. Without ignoring the negative cast of "confused" and "contradictory," we should note an opposing ("contradictory") current that moves the speaker. He appears "stepping with light feet." [...]

The rhythmic insistence of "sleep" works like a mantra—or an absolving prayer—as if the speaker, a sort of father confessor, sinner-forgiver, put to rest and "forgave" the faculties that stunt, block, or kill fruitful union. Larson calls Whitman's conjunctions "exaggerated juxtapositions" and claims that they "further emphasize a world closed off to all mediations." Instead, the enfolding of good and bad sets off the rhythmic movement toward a unity that the end of the poem will celebrate.

> —Carol Z. Whelan, "'Do I Contradict Myself?': Progression through Contraries in Walt Whitman's 'The Sleepers,'" *Walt Whitman Quarterly Review* 10, no. 1 (Summer 1992): pp. 25–27.

[In the excerpt below, R. W. French, University of Massachu-
setts, speaks of "The Sleepers" as a dream vision, a type of
poem that dates as far back as the early Middle Ages, in which
the poet embarks on a psychological journey, beginning in
confusion and ending with a vision of perfect harmony.]

"The Sleepers" has long been counted among the more obscure
poems of *Leaves of Grass*; it is, for example, the one poem that John
Burroughs, who began reading Whitman in 1858 or 1859, singled
out almost forty years later as being among those works in the *Leaves*
he did not yet understand. Yet Whitman **did** much to make his
meaning clear. "I wander all night in my vision," the poet proclaims
at the start; after which he passes on a journey of the mind, making
his way through varied experiences and recollections until he
reaches a state of enlightenment that allows him to declare, without
reservation, "The universe is duly in order, every thing is in its
place." As much as any Whitman poem, "The Sleepers" moves pur-
posefully toward a definite conclusion: the journey has meaning,
and no stage of it is merely accidental.

Much of the critical uncertainty about "The Sleepers" can be
resolved by recognizing its genre. Since the obvious is often overlooked, it is important that the obvious be stated: the poem is exactly
what it appears to be, and what Whitman says it is in the opening line,
a vision; more specifically, a dream vision. While it is not a definitive
representative of dream vision, any more than "Song of Myself" is a
definitive representative of epic, nevertheless it shares important
attributes with such works as "The Dream of the Rood," "The Pearl,"
The Divine Comedy, The Romance of the Rose, "The Book of the
Duchess," "The House of Fame," "The Parlement of Foules," *The
Vision of Piers Plowman, The Pilgrim's Progress*, "The Triumph of Life,"
and "The Fall of Hyperion." While these works are so diverse that no
generalization will readily apply to all of them, nevertheless it could be
argued that the characteristic dream vision begins in confusion and
ends in clarity; or at the very least that the dream experience significantly enhances the dreamer's understanding. Thus the dream vision
may be perceived as something of a gift, a sign of favor, the granting of
a boon that gives particular insight into essential matters and, in the
most ambitious of the genre—*The Divine Comedy* of course comes to

mind—into the center of the universe itself. In dream visions, then, the action that matters takes place within the dreamer's mind, which is left markedly changed by its experience. [. . .]

"The Sleepers" begins with the poet as mere dreamer, caught up in his own confusions, powerless, unable to act or to respond sympathetically to the world about him. His isolation is extreme; it imprisons him within the self, depriving him of the largeness of experience necessary to full existence. At best he is only half alive. When he moves out toward a loving relationship, when he responds sympathetically to suffering, his mind expands into imaginative possibility; there is a sense of wondrous release, as confusion opens out into knowledge. He begins, in short, to discover what it means to be a poet—or at least to be a poet such as Whitman would have, as envisioned most notably in "Song of Myself," but surely present in "The Sleepers" as well. By turning toward the needs of the suffering, the poet of "The Sleepers" leaves the self behind; and yet, perhaps paradoxically, by doing so he finds the means that liberate the self from bondage to its crippling sorrows and delusions. "The Universe," wrote Emerson in "The Poet," "is the externization of the soul." Who would discover one must discover the other.

From its initial confusion and distress the poem now leaps into ecstasy. "I am a dance," the poet proclaims; "play up there! the fit is whirling me fast!/ I am the ever-laughing." Everywhere the poet sees energy and vitality coursing through life; all about him hover the "nimble ghosts" who join him in boisterous conviviality: "Onward we move," he chants, "a gay gang of blackguards! with mirth-shouting music and wild-flapping pennants of joy!" Clearly, there has been a dramatic change of mood; in contrast to the sombre portrayal of life earlier in the poem, we turn now to uninhibited joy and abandon.

Confident, celebratory as though overcome by his newly-discovered powers of sympathy, the poet surges through other identities. "I am the actor, the actress, the voter, the politician," he proclaims. As he does so, however, a darker note begins to intrude. The initial enthusiasms turn out to have been premature and unearned; for the process of enlightenment is not yet complete. It lacks depth of understanding; there needs to be a firmer commitment to the complex and contradictory fullness of reality before it can be sustained. The poet's mind is not yet in a state to withstand the hostile pressures of experience; now, turning back to life's outcasts and unfortunates, he imagines himself "the exile, the criminal that stood in the box/ . . . the wasted or feeble person." The movement from joy back toward despair is psychologically right, as disillusion follows the fall from ecstasy; thus the poet's identification with the victims of life gains poignancy from the failed promise of hope.

Immediately after this identification, the poem appears to reverse itself, holding out the prospect of rapturous celebration as the poet becomes the woman whose lover has come: "I am she who adorn'd herself and folded her hair expectantly,/ My truant lover has come, and it is dark." Even here, however, there are ominous overtones. The lover is a "truant lover," unreliable and perhaps uncaring. The woman, so carefully adorned, appears vulnerable and exposed; and her role is largely passive, as she is the one who waits, who is received by the darkness and her lover, who resigns herself to the dusk, and who, at the end, follows and fades away.

Furthermore, this passage turns out to be not about the fulfillment of passion, but about its decline, if not its impossibility. There is anticipation of passionate love, and there is the falling away from it, but little is made of the actual experience, which is suggested only in retrospect, and then only in physical terms: "Darkness, you are gentler than my lover, his flesh was sweaty and panting,/ I feel the hot moisture yet that he left me." There is no sense of joy about the meeting, no rapturous outburst; rather, the woman appears to be used and abandoned. Not surprisingly, she turns to the darkness as substitute lover—a lover perhaps preferable for its gentleness:

> He whom I call answers me and takes the place of my lover,
> He rises with me silently from the bed.
> Darkness, you are gentler than my lover.

It may be that darkness is, finally, the only lover that matters, for darkness is inevitable: it can be trusted, for it will always be available, and it will turn no one away. In any case, the section ends (much like the "Ode to a Nightingale") in loss, and longing, and a sense of widening distance, as the woman fades away to emptiness. At the end she becomes yet one more representation of human life in all its transience and isolation.

—R. W. French, "Whitman's Dream Vision: A Reading of 'The Sleepers,'" *Walt Whitman Quarterly Review* 8, no. 1 (Summer 1990): p. 1, 5–7. ❀

MUTLU BLASING ON THE PROBLEM OF SELF IN "THE SLEEPERS"

[Mutlu Blasing is the author of such books as *American Poetry: The Rhetoric of Its Forms* and *Politics and Form in Post-Modern Poetry: O'Hara, Bishop, Ashbery & Merrill.* In the excerpt below, Blasing discusses how the contradictions of "The Sleepers" involves the poet's substituting his own identity for a new concept of self.]

Although 'The Sleepers' is one of Whitman's most beautiful and most problematic poems, it has only begun to receive critical attention, and the interpretations that it has received are remarkable for their variety. For example, Gay Wilson Allen and Charles T. Davis read the poem as an embodiment of the philosophic doctrine of reincarnation. James E. Miller, Jr., on the other hand, sees it as a 'vision' or a penetration into the 'world of dreams.' More recently, in a psychological study of Whitman's poetry, Edwin H. Miller regards 'The Sleepers' as not only an intensely personal 'confession' but 'a reenactment of ancient puberty rites.' Finally, R. W. Vince interprets the poem as a dramatization of the transcendence of evil through sympathy or love. [...]

Since 'The Sleepers' dramatizes the transcendence of personal identify in time and space, it is appropriately dominated by images of night, darkness, and sleep, all of which suggest a state of fluid, disembodied consciousness. In transcending identity, however, one negates the possibility of personal life at the same time that he transcends personal death. When consciousness rises above identity, time, space, and therefore death, the self as identity—as the only possible concretization of consciousness—has literally died. Accordingly, the night/darkness imagery reflects the paradoxical nature of self-transcendence, for the night signifies a force that is at once creative and destructive. Thus the night/darkness imagery is explicitly associated with death. Whitman's attitude toward death is itself similarly ambivalent. Whereas he welcomes death as the rebirth into spiritual life and hails it in 'Song of Myself' to be as 'lucky' as birth, he also exhibits, perhaps in spite of himself, an unqualified abhorrence of physical decay ('A Hand-Mirror') and death ('This Compost').

The paradoxical nature of self-transcendence, then, accounts for the dual significance of the images of night, darkness, and sleep.

Sleep is tentatively identified with death first in line 6: 'How solemn they look there, stretch'd and still.' 'Corpses' and 'gash'd bodies' in the following lines reinforce this identification. At the end of the first catalogue of sleepers, however, night is described in sexual terms: 'The night pervades them and infolds them.' By the third stanza of the section, then, night represents the source of both life and death, since 'infolds' clearly associates night with the womb. Moreover, in lines 46–59, darkness as the lover is a procreative force. In lines 68–69, however, darkness is associated with death, which here is not at all positive:

> (It seems to me that every thing in the light and air ought to be happy,
> Whoever is not in his coffin and the dark grave let him know that he has enough.)

Moreover, when the persona becomes a disembodied consciousness, he himself comes to be identified with the night:

> Now I pierce the darkness, new beings appear,
> The earth recedes from me into the night,
> I saw that it was beautiful, and I see that what is not the earth is beautiful.

With the receding of the earth, the persona is suspended in nothingness; totally disembodied, he is able now to encompass within himself the range of possible dreams. As a result, by dreaming 'all the dreams of the other dreamers,' he can 'become the other dreamers.' In his role of sleep-bringer, the persona was tentatively identified with the benevolent aspects of the night in lines 23–25. Furthermore, in lines 33–41 the sleepers' secrets, the nature of which is suggested by the sexual overtones of the passage, are revealed to the persona. Here again the persona is equated with the night, from which the sleepers can have no secrets. The persona's identification with the night continues in line 70: 'I descend my western course.'

The poet, therefore, not only assumes various individual identities and dramatizes their thoughts and actions, but becomes the medium or locus of these visions. For example, the persona becomes both the woman waiting for her lover and darkness itself, which is her lover. Thus the consciousness of the poet as 'night' is the lover of the woman—or the particular identity that the poet has now assumed. This passage is similar to Section 5 of 'Song of Myself,' where the relationship of the poet's soul to his body is presented in sexual terms. Furthermore, the persona is the mourning widow as well as the shroud that descends into the grave. In its identification with night and darkness, then, consciousness becomes itself a procreative yet destructive force.

Consciousness is similarly identified with water. In a stanza originally part of 'The Sleepers' but omitted by Whitman in 1881, water imagery was introduced first to signify sexual knowledge:

> O hot-cheek'd and blushing! O foolish hectic!
> O for pity's sake, no one must see me now! my clothes were stolen while I was abed,
> Now I am thrust forth, where shall I run?
> Pier that I saw dimly last night, when I look'd from the windows!
> Pier out from the main, let me catch myself with you, and stay—I will not chafe you,
> I feel ashamed to go naked about the world.
> I am curious to know where my feet stand and what this is flooding me, childhood or manhood—and the hunger that crosses the bridge between.

Here the night merges with water, and darkness and water—both sexual forces of creation and destruction—are identified with the consciousness of the persona. Although this is a remarkable passage in its dream-like texture, it is not hard to see why Whitman chose to exclude it, for such a passage would lead to a misunderstanding of the 'vision' of the poem as strictly a dream-experience. The passage is significant, however, insofar as it dramatizes the fear of losing one's identify—the 'film' of appearances—and standing naked before others.

—Mutlu Blasing, "'The Sleepers': The Problem of the Self in Whitman," *Walt Whitman Review* 21, no. 2 (Summer 1975): pp. 111–114.

Thematic Analysis of
"Crossing Brooklyn Ferry"

"Crossing Brooklyn Ferry," first published in the 1856 edition of *Leaves of Grass*, is one of Whitman's most accomplished poems, demonstrating a mastery of poetic power. Its form is one simple, unified scene, that of a ferry shuttling back and forth between Brooklyn and Manhattan; it is nevertheless a brilliant example of Whitman's ability to turn an everyday experience, "crowds of men and women attired in the usual costumes," into an imaginative experience.

In section 1, amid the background of the flood tide, the poet states his purpose: to explore through meditations the previously undiscovered possibilities of the anonymous crowds that daily cross the river:

> On the ferry-boats the hundreds and hundreds that cross, returning home, are more curious to me than you suppose.

By showing those previously undiscovered possibilities through the power of his mind, the poet appoints himself spiritual and poetic guide.

In section 2, Whitman continues his role as captain of this voyage. He installs himself as an unseen, divine, impalpable presence and denies the death-dealing effects of time by disallowing commonplace forms of expression. The poet is now free to see beyond the horizons.

In section 3, Whitman continues to direct the vision of the voyage, in which the voyagers and the poet are simultaneously "refreshed by the gladness of the river and the bright flow." As the floating motion of river allows these everyday burdens of time and place to be suspended, the passengers are able to stand still on a ferry, effortlessly transported: "Just as you stand and lean on the rail, yet hurry with the swift current, I stood yet was hurried." Such descriptions of the river as "the scallop-edged waves in the twilight, the ladled cups, the frolicsome crests and glistening" make Whitman's artistic transformation of a boat ride even more of a tour de force. The poet exerts enormous imaginative power to celebrate freedom from the mortal concerns of time, space, and even death, floating like seagulls "with motionless wings." This experience is reiterated in the few brief statements of section 4.

Section 5 begins with a question: "What is the count of the scores or hundreds of years between us?" and repeats the phrase, "it avails not." Having removed the concepts of time and place, Whitman seeks a common denominator, namely, the shared human experiences of self-doubt and loss of identity: "I too felt the curious abrupt questionings stir within me,/ . . . I too had receiv'd identity by my body."

Section 6 continues the same questioning, including the human fallibility that the poet shares with all men. "It is not upon you alone the dark patches fall,/ The dark threw its patches down upon me also." The poet admits guilt:

> Nor is it you alone who know what it is to be evil,
> I am he who knew what it was to be evil,
> I too knitted the old knot of contrariety,
> Blabb'd, blush'd, resented, lied, stole, grudg'd,
> Had guile, anger, lust, hot wishes I dared not speak.

His guilt becomes a source of strength as he further meditates on the cause for his wrongdoing. The poet comes to see himself as a victim, having suffered endless rounds of meanness, rejection, and refusals. Whitman's answer to the question of how to live one's life returns to one of his favorite metaphors—that man is an actor on the stage with the power to define himself and the image he projects to the rest of the world:

> Play'd the part that still look back on the actor or actress,
> The same old role, the role that is what we make it, as great as we like,
> Or as small as we like, or both great and small.

Section 7 allows the poet to bring himself even closer, following his confession of shared guilt and fallibility with all mankind.

In section 8, the poet reminds us that he possesses a unique communication with the divine: "What gods can exceed these that clasp me by the hand, and with voices I love call me promptly and loudly by my nighest name as I approach?" He repeats his earlier promise of newfound freedom over the tyranny of the everyday world; this promise becomes vaguer and more distant, requiring greater faith:

> We understand then do we not?
> What I promis'd without mentioning it, have you not accepted?
> What the study could not teach—what the preaching could not
>   accomplish is accomplish'd, is it not?

In section 9, the poet addresses the river and directs it to carry out its divine ministry. Again his advice is to assume the role of the actor, to take control of language by suspending its harmful effects, to avoid answering the questions through skillful maneuverings, and in assuming this responsibility to provide a support to those who are unable:

> Live, old life! Play the part that looks back on the actor or actress!
> Play the old role, the role that is great or small according as one makes it! . . .
> Consider, you who peruse me, whether I may not in unknown ways be looking upon you.
> Be firm, rail over the river, to support those who lean idly, yet haste with the hasting current. ❀

Critical Views on
"Crossing Brooklyn Ferry"

MARK KINKEAD-WEEKES ON WHITMAN'S
ORCHESTRATION OF TIME

[Mark Kinkead-Weekes is the author of such books as *D. H. Lawrence: Triumph to Exile* and *William Golding: A Critical Study*. In the excerpt below, Kindead-Weekes discusses how Whitman successfully orchestrates time in "Crossing Brooklyn Ferry."]

'Crossing Brooklyn Ferry' is a deeply democratic poem in the sense that it springs naturally and unforced from the experience of anyone who has ever crossed on a big-city ferry—a marvellously complex and convincing work built out of the very ordinary. From the beginning it is concrete and specific, set matter-of-factly in space and time: the flood tide, the sun half an hour from setting, the hundreds of people sharing the experience, the people who will cross years hence. The poem seems to grow spontaneously, unmanipulated, with no showing off of the poet, or his powers, and yet from the start there is a quiet declaration that the 'usual' may be more extraordinary and meaningful than one supposes.

The second section allows the setting and the crowds to sustain the individual poet. He and all the other individuals are alone, 'disintegrated,' yet part of the 'scheme'; his actions in walking the streets and being borne on the flood are 'similitudes' of both past and future; they have happened before and will happen again; and this gives them a glory in their ordinariness for they connect him with 'certainty of others.' The tense breaks into the future, in the calm and naturally justified conviction that others *will* do and see just as he does and sees.

In the third section Whitman enacts just this in enacting the crossing. In closely observed visual detail he brings the scene alive: the gulls wheeling above in the last of the sunlight, the low sun aureoling the reflection of his head in the water, the haze on the hills, the shipping coming in from the bay, the activity in the docks, the light fading, the fires from the foundry chimneys casting flickering lights on housetops and the chasms of the streets. There seems little to say about this section except to point to the vividness, the conviction that this is just what he saw, and what one would see essentially oneself. Difference of place and date are insignificant.

So when he declares his love for Brooklyn and Manhattan and the stately river, it is matter of fact; and we accept equally his feeling for the others crossing with him, for the affection of the whole portrayal includes them. We can even accept quite simply that imagining the future the same as his present has brought him 'near' to those who will look back on him—ourselves—because he looked forward to them—'The time will come, though I stop here to-day and to-night.' This gives a strange yet simple feeling, for of course the time has come and Walt Whitman has stopped . . . in a sense.

But in a sense this is not so. In the fifth section the poem begins to stir and grow curiously. For it was with the body that is now dead— as he foresaw, putting himself into the past—that Walt Whitman was himself in his personal identity, 'struck from the float.' It was in his body that he was what he had called in another poem a simple separate person. And it was also through the physical imagination that he is able to enter past and future. In the sixth section he writes a self-analysis quite free from posturing and attitudinizing; simply emphasizing how it was his life in the body that gave him the ordinary experience of humanity, the evil as well as the good, the friendship and the reticence. (Perhaps Whitman's homosexuality adds a level of meaning here, but one would distort by emphasizing it, because he is stressing the common experience of all human beings.) [. . .]

So he has earned the right in the final section to celebrate the crossing again, and all the things he 'saw,' in that continuous present tense and imperative mood that are his favourite modes of expression, because the limitation of finite time is abolished and control is assured. 'Flow on,' he cries, 'flow and ebb . . . frolic on . . . drench . . . cross . . . stand up . . . throb . . . suspend here and everywhere, eternal float of solution . . . gaze . . . sound out . . . live,' and so *on*. The rich vitality is urged on into continuous active life; and the imperative takes place both in his time scheme and in ours.

—Mark Kinkead-Weekes, "Walt Whitman Passes the Full-Stop by . . . ," in *Nineteenth Century American Poetry*, ed. A. Robert Lee (Totowa, N.J.: Barnes & Noble Books, 1985): pp. 56–59.

ROGER ASSELINEAU ON THE SUSPENSION OF TIME IN "CROSSING BROOKLYN FERRY"

[Roger Asselineau is the author of several books on Walt Whitman, among them *The Evolution of Walt Whitman: The Development of a Personality.* In the excerpt below, Asselineau discusses the images and structures which create the paradox of stasis in motion and the suspension of time in "Crossing Brooklyn Ferry."]

With "Crossing Brooklyn Ferry" (first published in 1856 as "Sun-Down Poem"), Whitman began not a new form but a more organized structure of his poems. Although this poem is neither a description nor a narration of a physical trip across the East River to Manhattan, the motif of such a trip (like Thoreau's "week" on the two rivers) gives the poet the real subject of his poem, which is his meditations on defying time by preserving his transitory experiences in art—the theme of some of Shakespeare's sonnets and of Keats's "Ode on a Grecian Urn." But, except for the theme, Whitman's poem in no way resembles any of Shakespeare's sonnets or Keats's "Ode"; and the difference is in the form, structure, and diction.

"Crossing Brooklyn Ferry" begins in reminiscence—the historical present:

> Flood-tide below me! I see you face to face!
> Clouds of the west—sun there half an hour high—
> I see you face to face. [...]

As the poet invokes the memory of the river at flood tide half an hour before sunset (a symbol of death), he feels himself to be again one of the crowd on the ferry and projects the memory backward and forward in time, both reliving and anticipating his experience as an integral part in the unity of boat, tide, crowd, and the two shores; and he can easily imagine an endless repetition of the experience. Ergo, by preserving the memory in a poem that will continue to be read long after his death, he will have caused time to stand still, or cease to exist. His creative problem is finding images, rhythms, and grammatical structures to *express* this paradox of stasis in motion. He succeeds not by the use of new prosodic or linguistic techniques but in adapting those of "Song of Myself." At a glance, the poem is seen to have the same strophe units based on a group of parallel statements (ending with a period), the same use of a repeated word or phrase at the beginning of the line. And variation of the rhythms is achieved by shifting accentual patterns. But these are subtly adapted to the theme and tone of the ferry allegory—for it is an allegory of life and art, or life turned into art. [. . .]

Having no narration, section 2 does not progress in time or place, but the succession of images—ferry gates, flowing tide, shores, ships, Brooklyn Heights, the sun low on the horizon, etc.—give an illusion of motion. Though the time of the poem is half an hour before sunset, the day and the clock-hour are irrelevant because in section 3 the season is both winter ("Twelfth-month") and summer; it is no-time and all-time, which is the theme of the section. "It avails not, time or place—distance avails not. . . " This paradox is symbolized in sky and water, in the circling gulls, "high in the air, floating with motionless wings, oscillating their bodies,"

> Saw the slow-wheeling circles and the gradual edging
>   toward the south,
> Saw the reflection of the summer sky in the water,
> Had my eyes dazzled by the shimmering track of beams,
> Look'd at the fine centrifugal spokes of light round
>   the shape of my head in the sunlit water.

The movement of the poem is centrifugal. The trip is from portal to portal, and the experiencing "I" sees his own halo in the water, which also ebbs and flows. The passengers, too, who cross over to Manhattan will later return to Brooklyn, perhaps make the round trip many times, as the poet *has* done and *will* do. Life and death are also circular. Individuals emerge from the "float" and return to it.

> I too had been struck from the float forever held in solution,
> I too had receiv'd identity by my body.

"Float," a metaphor for the salt water (or ocean) in the East River, is obviously symbolical, whether it be interpreted as the equivalent of Emerson's Over-Soul, Chari's "cosmic consciousness," or Edwin Miller's womb and amniotic fluid. The word is repeated in line 106 as "eternal float of solution" and is invoked to "suspend." In the chemical sense, "solution" means a fluid in which the ingredients remain dissolved and seemingly unified. However, in the context of the poet's invocations to the river to "flow," the waves to "frolic," the clouds to "drench" with their splendor (not *shine* or *radiate* but *drench*, like a soaking rain), the masts and hills to "stand up," the brain to "throb," we would expect the word "suspend" to have a strongly active, positive meaning: such as remain capable of producing new living "identities" to continue the process of birth-out-of-death.

That the poet is calling for more life, more vibrant activity, more sense gratifications, is implied in the succeeding lines in which he commands the "loving and thirsty eyes" to *gaze*, the voices of young men to *sound out* and call him (the poet) by his "nighest name." In the same spirit, he also feels his kinship with common, average humanity, including their weaknesses and perversities. In spite of human faults, all lives have emerged from the "eternal float" and each person who looks into the shimmering water will see "fine spokes of light" haloing his head, just as the poet has.

—Roger Asselineau, *A Reader's Guide to Walt Whitman* (Syracuse, N.Y.: Syracuse University Press, 1970): pp. 186–90.

Manuel Villar Raso on Musical Structure in "Crossing Brooklyn Ferry"

[Manuel Villar Raso is a professor of American literature at the University of Granada and has written several novels. In the excerpt below, Raso discusses the unity of theme in "Crossing Brooklyn Ferry," which supports the theme of a "universality of experience."]

Originally titled "Sun-Down Poem" when it was published in 1856, this was Thoreau's favorite among Whitman's poems. It is sometimes said to be Whitman's most unified work, but the structure again is musical.

Certainly the kind of diversity of imagery and theme that we experience in *Leaves of Grass* is avoided in the unity of "Brooklyn Ferry". To begin with, it is an extremely concrete poem, its images detailing a specific experience in a specific time and place. They give it the kind of credibility that many of the more generalized sections of "Song" lack. But the poet is concerned with more than an individual experience; in this single event, he sees a kind of universality of experience.

This universality, clearly, does not involve the act of crossing a particular river on a particular ferry. Indeed, the ferry no longer runs, but this does not limit the application of Whitman's thesis. Speaking to all men in future times, he asserts that they, too, will make this journey:

> Others will enter the gates of the ferry and cross from shore to shore.
> (sec. 2: 13)

The shores are more than Brooklyn and Manhattan: they are the shores of birth and death; the ferry is human life; and the river is not the East River but the river of time. It is thus that he can speak of the universality of his experience and his thought.

But the importance for us is the structure of "Crossing Brooklyn Ferry" and this structure, like that of his best works, is the musical structure of the expression of individual themes, the examination of them separately and in various combinations and the final statement of them, enriched by the new contexts in which they have been seen. The wealth of concrete imagery gives credence to the generalized statements and the poem is organized in part with an enormous amount of original rhyme.

Something similar happens with his second great poem, "Out of the Cradle Endlessly Rocking," the great masterpiece of the new America, the remarkable genesis of the poet, a narrative reminiscence of a childhood experience, with its drama of the boy setting forth as a bard listening by the seaside to the mockingbird's carol of lonesome love and the sea's answering hiss of death.

The major images of the poem are the boy, the bird and the sea. Its structure, again, is musical: the bird songs are arias of fulfillment and frustration, and much of the tone is that of the recitative. But, since I intend to analyse in more depth and detail his third great poem, "When Lilacs Last in the Dooryard Bloom'd", a poem whose musical and symphonic structure is most clear, I leave out "Out of the Cradle" for a better occasion.

—Manuel Villar Raso, "Musical Structure of Whitman's Poems," in *Utopia in the Present Tense* (Rome: University of Macerata, 1994): pp. 194–95. ⓟ

SUSAN STROM ON THE BIBLICAL "FACE TO FACE" IN "CROSSING BROOKLYN FERRY"

[In the excerpt below, Susan Strom discusses the significance of the biblical phrase "face to face," here focusing on Jacob's confrontation with God.]

In 'Crossing Brooklyn Ferry' the structure of Biblical reference depends primarily on the phrase 'face to face,' the image with which Whitman begins the poem. Carried through the poem both concretely and obliquely, the opening image of the poet standing between the flood-tide and the sky, mediating between these two elements and translating their significance, is the thematic and imagistic basis of the poem. The image itself is one of unity in opposition; it is as such that a complete investigation of the indirect and direct meanings of this phrase as it appears in six distinct Biblical passages, and as these passages relate to the poem, must be examined.

The six Biblical passages all deal with some form of the prophetic vision or the prophetic experience. Within this framework, however, the passages have varying degrees of relevance to the poem as a whole. The passages may be divided into two groups, the first of which relates to the poem in a non-specific, indirect or background capacity, while the second may be related directly to the thematic and imagistic structure of the poem.

The first group is primarily concerned with the general conception and definition of prophecy and the nature of the prophet's role; this can then be related to Whitman's conception of himself as poet-prophet as it is revealed in 'Crossing Brooklyn Ferry.' Contained in this group are four Old Testament passages: Genesis 32:30, Deuteronomy 5:4, Deuteronomy 34:10, and Judges 6:22.

Genesis 32:30, which deals with Jacob's physical and spiritual confrontation with God, may be said to be the archetypal example of the prophetic experience:

> And Jacob called the name of the place Peniel: for I have seen God face to face, and my life is preserved.

In this incident, an aspect of prophecy other than what Whitman described as the 'bubbling up and pouring forth' of spirit is revealed. Here, Jacob is not overflowing with God's message; rather, he is seen in the act of wrestling with a physical embodiment of the divine spirit. Fundamental to this aspect of the prophetic role is the perception of the prophet both as combatant and as namer. Expressed in the terms of the poem, the conflict between man and God may be seen as a battle of consciousness in which the body must actively confront the soul in order to advance into a higher state of awareness. The essence of this awareness is a comprehension of the separate and yet conjoined functions of the body and the spirit of man.

The face-to-face confrontation which takes place between God and Jacob results in the creation and the naming of an entirely new entity which is born of the battle: it is in this passage that Jacob becomes Israel, and the man, in union with his God, is transformed from an individual to a people. It is through this direct conflict that the one in the present becomes the many of the future. The existence of the sense of illimitable future contained within a seemingly finite instant of time, physical being, and experience relates directly to the underlying concept of time, being and experience which is the basis of 'Crossing Brooklyn Ferry.'

Jacob's new future—the fulfillment of God's promise to Abraham—is concretized and realized by the act of changing names. This verbalization of a new awareness and a new reality is fundamental to the rhetorical structure of Whitman's poem; also, in stanza 8, where the reader is both asked and commanded to articulate his comprehension of the poetic experience it is particularly significant. In both cases, the act of naming or articulating is an Adamic act of creative synthesis which fuses the symbolic name with the concrete spiritual reality.

—Susan Strom, "'Face to Face': Whitman's Biblical Reference in 'Crossing Brooklyn Ferry,'" *Walt Whitman Review* 24, no. 1 (March 1978): pp. 8–9.

Thematic Analysis of
"Out of the Cradle Endlessly Rocking"

Originally entitled "A Child's Reminiscence" in an 1859 manu-script, "Out of the Cradle Endlessly Rocking" was published in 1860, five years after the first edition of *Leaves of Grass*. It is one of Whitman's seashore poems, concerned with childhood memories of the sea and the beach, memories that are at the center of the tragic in life. The poem is told as two narratives: the story of the mournful mockingbird and the parallel story of a boy's relation-ship with that bird as part of his own process of maturation. It is interspersed with lyrical sections, in which music and song create both the background for a full understanding of the two narratives and the focal point towards which the poet's energies are directed.

The poem begins with a small boy listening to a mockingbird sing the sad song of the loss of its mate, then takes us through the child's maturing process towards his becoming both a man and a poet—the solitary singer who will subsume the mockingbird's function:

> O you singer solitary, singing by yourself, projecting me,
> O solitary me listening, never more shall I cease perpetuating you.

The poem begins with an image of a "cradle endlessly rocking"; it is the cradle we come from and we revisit as adults in an attempt to understand ourselves. The persistence of memory is implied from the outset in the sounds of a cradle mimicking the sounds of the ebb and flow of the ocean's tide. The first stanza shows a yearning for a communion with nature, specifically the poet's longing to form a sympathetic relationship with the mockingbird:

> Out of the Ninth-month midnight,
> Over the sterile sands and the fields beyond, where the child leaving
> his bed wander'd alone, bareheaded, barefoot,
> Down from the shower'd halo, . . .
> From those beginning notes of yearning and love there in the mist.

This is an adult voice speaking, reflecting on his own childhood, a man transported back, to become like the mockingbird:

> Borne hither, ere all eludes me, hurriedly,
> A man, yet by these tears a little boy again,

> Throwing myself on the sand, confronting the waves,
> I chanter of pains and joys, uniter of here and hereafter.

There is a very strong spirituality infused throughout this poem in such lines as "up from the mystic play," with a pun on the word "mystic," referring to both the mist of the ocean spray as well as to the idea of mystery or hidden meaning yet to be discovered.

The next stanza brings the details of the poet's childhood into focus. Whitman refers to Long Island as "Paumanok," its original Indian name, underscoring the poet's desire to return to his origins. The child is a student of nature dedicated to careful, but reverently distant, observance:

> And every day I, a curious boy, never too close, never disturbing them,
> Cautiously peering, absorbing, translating.

What follows is a brief interlude of the song of the mockingbird, continuing

> Till of a sudden,
> May-be kill'd, unknown to her mate,
> One forenoon the she-bird crouch's not on the nest,
> Nor return'd that afternoon, nor the next,
> Nor ever appear'd again.

Speculation on the death of the she-bird elicits pathos in the pronounced suffering of the male mockingbird. Now, as the child gazes on the "solitary guest from Alabama," he sees a scene of mourning and the burden that death places on the loved ones who survive.

Whitman proclaims himself the self-appointed prophet and spiritual guide to all mankind; he alone is qualified to receive the hidden spiritual message of his beloved mockingbird: "He pour'd forth the meanings which I of all men knew." This interruption in the narrative of the grieving bird forces a shift of attention back to the poet. The next sixty lines become the poet's singing voice, operatic and celebratory:

> O throat! O trembling throat!
> Sound clearer through the atmosphere!
> Pierce the woods, the earth,
> Somewhere listening to catch you must be the one I want.

The boy has now appropriated the complaint of the forlorn bird as his own plaintive voice calling out to his lost love:

> With this just-sustain'd note I announce myself to you,
> This gentle call is for you my love, for you.

In the next section of the poem, the bird's voice fades. It is the matured poet, and not the grieving bird, who is responsible for the dramatic representation of the mockingbird's plight:

> And already a thousand singers, a thousand songs, clear, louder and more sorrowful than yours,
> A thousand warbling echoes have started to life within me, never to die.

Whitman addresses the bird, asking whom his song is directed to. Then he answers the question himself: The song is meant for the poet and the message is death. Though the poem acknowledges death, death is not to be feared: "Lisp'd to me the low and delicious word death."

The meaning of the poem is found in the poet's identification with the mockingbird and the merging of their two voices until only the voice of the child-poet is heard. The child-poet has reached maturity; he will assume the same burden as his cherished mockingbird; he is the poet, responsible for singing the lament of the lost lover: "O solitary me listening, never more shall I cease perpetuating you." ✦

Critical Views on
"Out of the Cradle Endlessly Rocking"

JOHN T. IRWIN ON EGYPTIAN HIEROGLYPHICS
IN "OUT OF THE CRADLE"

[John T. Irwin is author of *The Mystery to a Solution: Poe,
Borges and the Analytic Detective Story* and *American Hiero-
glyphics: The Symbol of the Egyptian Hieroglyphics in the
American Renaissance.* In the excerpt below, Irwin discusses
Whitman's interest in the nineteenth-century renewal of
Egyptology and his incorporation of those ideas throughout
Leaves of Grass, including a specific discussion of "Out of
the Cradle Endlessly Rocking."]

I have discussed at some length hieroglyphic Bibles and the tradition
of the hieroglyphical interpretation of the Bible represented by Swedenborg and Oegger because there is reason to believe that at one
point Whitman conceived of *Leaves of Grass* as a kind of hieroglyphic Bible. The evidence is circumstantial but ample. To begin
with, there is Whitman's interest in the hieroglyphics and Egyptology, the fact that he called his major symbol "a uniform hieroglyphic," and that in *A Backward Glance* he implicitly compared
Leaves of Grass, "his *carte visite* to the coming generations," to Champollion's hieroglyphic grammar. Indeed, Whitman may have had in
mind Emerson's remark that for Swedenborg the world was a
"grammar of hieroglyphs." Next, we know that as late as June 1857
Whitman considered his ongoing work on *Leaves of Grass* as "the
Great Construction of the New Bible." The Bible was, of course, the
major influence on Whitman's prosody, shaping his cadenced verse
with its repetitions and parallelisms. Further, many of the elements
found in the format of the hieroglyphic Bible are to be found in
Leaves of Grass as well. In addition to the figure of the cipher and the
key, there is the Adamic motif of calling things by their right names,
that is, by their original names. In characterizing Champollion's
achievement as the construction of "a grammar" from "the old car-
touches," Whitman emphasizes the central role of proper names in
the decipherment of the hieroglyphics; for in the metaphysical tradition the authentic "proper names" are right, original names, and
thus Champollion's decipherment of the Egyptian hieroglyphics by

means of proper names is itself a kind of hieroglyphical representation, a veiled prefiguration, of the correct method for deciphering the hieroglyphs of nature. According to this tradition, when the language of words derived from the original language of objects, the words that derived first and that are still closest to that original language were concrete nouns—the proper names of physical objects. Emerson refers to this notion in *Nature* when he remarks, "Every word which is used to express a moral or intellectual fact, if traced to its root, is found to be borrowed from some material appearance." And this concept of the noun also underlies Thoreau's choice of the nouns "lobe" and "leaf" to analyze into their hieroglyphic radicals. [. . .]

In "Out of the Cradle Endlessly Rocking," the poet travels by means of his song back to his own childhood (and thus toward man's ultimate origin, "the cosmic float," symbolized by the sea) in order to hear once again the song of the bird calling to its lost mate. And he realizes that the singing of the bird has a double meaning: it is at once an image of the world calling to the separated self of the poet and an image of the poet singing in order to "expire," to breath himself into the world:

> Demon or bird! (said the boy's soul,)
> Is it indeed toward your mate you sing? or is it really to me?
> For I, that was a child, my tongue's use sleeping, now I have heard
> you,
> Now in a moment I know what I am for, I awake
> And already a thousand singers, a thousand songs, clearer, louder and
> more sorrowful than yours,
> A thousand warbling echoes have started to life within me, never to
> die.
> O you singer solitary, singing by yourself, projecting me,
> O solitary me listening, never more shall I cease
> perpetuating you.

In Whitman's idealized conception of song, the musical component of poetry, by raising spoken language to that condition in which its sonic form is its content (in which vocal expiration is a return to origin, to that original interpenetration of sign and meaning), transforms spoken language into the audible equivalent of that original language of natural signs in which the form of the pictographic physical object was transparently its meaning. Thus in Whitman's poetry, song is presented as the mode of the poet's return to a childlike simplicity of character, to those radically simple, written characters of the original language of natural signs through which the poet's character is expressed. Whitman aims, through the fusing power of song, to turn the phallic tree of spoken language back into the cosmic tree of the language of natural signs within his own cosmic written self, the Walt Whitman whose song (*Leaves of Grass*) *is* his poetic self.

—John T. Irwin, "Whitman: Hieroglyphic Bibles and Phallic Songs," in *American Hieroglyphics: The Symbol of the Egyptian Hieroglyphics in the American Renaissance* (Baltimore and London: The Johns Hopkins University Press, 1980): pp. 31–32, 39–40.

JANET S. ZEHR ON THE ROLE OF MEMORY IN "OUT OF THE CRADLE"

[Janet S. Zehr, of Brandeis University, discusses the role of memory as a descriptive category for analyzing the various levels of time as Whitman takes us through his act of remembering.]

As Wordsworth suggests, the poet is thinking and expressing himself just as other people do, only better. In the readings of Pearce and Fussell are some implicit assumptions that I would like to make explicit. The poem is at least in part about memory and the way men's and women's minds, of which the poet's mind is the apotheosis, re-shape the events of the past. This re-shaping constantly alters time so that our conventional divisions of time—past, present, and future—are not quite adequate. In examining time in "Out of the Cradle," I can see a passage-way between the box in which I've placed Pearce and Fussell, stressing the workings of a poetic mind, and the one in which I've placed those who see Whitman as a prophet working with cosmic paradoxes and re-shaping our notions of the universe. As Whitman goes through the ordinary human act of remembering, he breaks down time barriers, showing us how we all are "uniter[s] of here and hereafter." [. . .]

Examining more specifically the workings of memory in "Out of the Cradle" reveals more ways in which various levels of time are blended. Whitman initially encouraged the idea that the poem was about the process of memory by entitling the poem "A Child's Reminiscence." Although a woman who heard the poem read by Whitman said the events were, as far as she knew, based on real experiences, we certainly will never know. Whitman surely asks of us, however, that we accept the fictional situation which involves a man looking back on childhood events.

In the poem, Whitman begins playing with time immediately. The rhythms of the long initial sentence—"Out of the," "Down from the," "Up from the"—create new poetic rhythms, new patterns in time. As Lynen says, the present participles of the same sentence —"rocking," "twining and twisting," "twittering," "revisiting"— create an endless present that need not be linked to any specific moment. The adult poet states that he is undergoing a transformation in time: "A man, yet by these tears a little boy again"and that he has the ability to unite "here and hereafter." In the next stanza, he begins "Once Paumanok," but, without any verb to indicate what happened "once," goes on to describe what happened not "once" but "every day."

This "once" clearly works as a story-telling convention and may not be as illogical as it first appears. It illustrates, however, the most striking type of time dislocation in the poem. The process of remembering and the tricks with time it involves are most obvious in the confusion between events that were repeated and those that occurred only once. [. . .]

Whitman says this song was sung and/or interpreted by the boy over and over again: "And *every day* I, a curious boy, never too close, never disturbing them,/ Cautiously peering, absorbing, translating" (italics added). The song proceeds, however, word for word:

> Shine! shine! shine!
> Pour down your warmth, great sun!
> While we bask, we two together.

This seemingly spontaneous bird song could not have been sung in precisely the same way *every day*. Nor would the boy have understood or translated the song in precisely this way every day. The man remembers one particular time that best represents what happened in more or less the same way every day. Or, perhaps more accurately, the man/poet in the present constructs one moment, a composite moment that may have very little relation to what actually occurred, that can relay the emotions of many more or less similar moments in the past. The poem seems to represent the process of remembering, quite apart from the process of making a poem from a memory, very accurately. We as ordinary human beings can think only of a representative "one time" or construct a composite memory of a time that never really existed at all.

—Janet S. Zehr, "The Act of Remembering in 'Out of the Cradle Endlessly Rocking,'" *Walt Whitman Quarterly Review* 1, no. 1 (September 1983): pp. 21–23.

WILLIAM F. MAYHAN ON WHITMAN'S CONCEPT OF MUSIC

[William F. Mayhan, of the University of Missouri, St. Louis, discusses how understanding Whitman's concept of music is an essential key to understanding the complexity of the poem, as it both provides structure and plays a symbolic role.]

When Walt Whitman first published "Out of the Cradle Endlessly Rocking" (then called "A Child's Reminiscence") in the Christmas Eve 1859 edition of the New York *Saturday Press*, he described the poem as "a curious warble." He went on to observe that "the purport of this wild and plaintive song, well-enveloped, and eluding definition, is positive and unquestionable, like the effect of music. The piece will bear reading many times—perhaps, indeed, only comes forth, as from recesses, by many repetitions." Later, when defending the poem against a published attack charging it with meaninglessness, Whitman explained that his organizational strategy "was strictly the method of the Italian Opera." By linking his poem so closely and specifically to music, Whitman offers a vital clue not only to the poem's unorthodox structure, but also to its meaning. It seems odd, indeed, that so blatant a clue has for so long been largely overlooked. [. . .]

The particular need for an investigation of the musical aspects of this specific poem, I believe, stems from the fact that in it, music plays not only a structural role, but also a symbolic one. In "Out of the Cradle Endlessly Rocking," Whitman blends his experience of music (as heard) with his philosophical conceptions of the nature and meaning of music in a marriage of matter and form that is itself the essence of music. This investigation will involve three major steps: an outline of Whitman's general attitude towards music, its nature and its communicative possibilities; a suggestion of possible sources for these attitudes; and finally, an investigation of how Whitman's conception of music relates to both the structure and meaning of "Out of the Cradle Endlessly Rocking."

During the late 1840s and throughout the 1850s, Whitman was an active concert- and opera-goer. His position as a reporter for the Brooklyn *Daily Eagle* allowed him many chances to put his musical experiences and reactions into print. Since he was not schooled in the technical aspects of music theory, Whitman's reviews of musical events focused mainly on purely personal reactions. This selection from an 1851 "Letter from Paumanok" is indicative of the kind of free-wheeling, impressionistic response Whitman had to musical performance:

> Have you not, in like manner, while listening to the well-played music of some band like Maretzek's, felt an overwhelming desire for measureless sound—a sublime orchestra of myriad orchestras—a colossal volume of harmony, in which the thunder might roll in its proper place; and above it, the vast, pure Tenor,—identity of the Creative Power itself—rising through the universe, until the boundless and unspeakable capacities of that mystery, the human soul, should be filled to the uttermost, and the problem of human cravingness be satisfied and destroyed?
>
> Of this sort are the promptings of good music upon me.

This response in many ways embodies the kind of attitude Whitman would hold toward music throughout his life: the poet almost always connects his experiences of music to an intuitive experience of the innermost realm of human nature. Music becomes the symbol for a kind of deep, universal order, an order which alone can fill the "boundless and unspeakable capacities" of the human soul. As music criticism, of course, this is woefully subjective and inadequate (although rather typical of nineteenth century responses to music); but as an indication of the kind of meaning Whitman ascribed to music, it is telling indeed. Music (and ultimately only music) holds the solution to the enigma of man in the world; it alone can "satisfy" and "destroy" the separateness man inevitably feels in the fact of the otherness of the world—and can replace this feeling of separateness with a "colossal volume of harmony."

That this mystical reaction to the power of music remains terribly abstract is for Whitman an inevitable consequence of the nature of musical language itself. Music communicates directly that which words can only obliquely describe.

—William F. Mayhan, "The Idea of Music in 'Out of the Cradle End-lessly Rocking,'" *Walt Whitman Quarterly Review* 13, no. 3 (Winter 1996): pp. 113–14.

A. James Wohlpart on the Boy-Poet's Knowledge

[In the excerpt below, A. James Wohlpart discusses the imagery of the boy-poet's knowledge in the early sections of the poem.]

The conflation of voices in "Out of the Cradle Endlessly Rocking," occurring primarily through Whitman's conflation of time in the poem, has led critics to assume that the boy-poet at the end of the unfolding drama is the same as the mature poet who speaks the opening stanza. For instance, Leo Spitzer concludes that once the boy hears the word spoken by the sea, the word "death," he discovers the "*meaning* of life, which is death, [and] he is no longer the boy of the beginning. . . . He has become the poet, the 'uniter of here and hereafter'" Gay Wilson Allen similarly concludes, in *A Reader's Guide to Walt Whitman,* that 'What the poem is really about is how the boy became a man and a poet through the childhood initiation into the mystery of death and maternity." Even while analyzing the cluster as a whole, Robin Fast comes to a similar conclusion. Fast claims that, at the end of the poem, the outsetting bard "reconciles himself to death" because he realizes that "death cannot truly separate the dead from the living, and life is part of a larger reality which includes all." The conclusion that most critics have reached is that "Out of the Cradle" shows not only the awakening of the poet but also his full maturity, his full knowledge of one of his major themes, at this very same moment of awakening.

More recently, however, critics have suggested that the boy-poet's knowledge at the end of the poem is not as complete as that which the mature poet attains some years later; indeed, it is only the knowledge that the mature poet attains which allows him to recreate the scene with some semblance of meaning. In his cursory analysis of the *Sea-Drift* cluster, which focuses on "Out of the Cradle," James Perrin Warren claims that "'Out of the Cradle' does not complete the story of the poet's spiritual birth and growth." Rather, Whitman presents two distinct voices in the poem, that of the outsetting bard and that of the mature poet, each representing different levels of maturity and knowledge. An attempt to separate these voices in "Out of the Cradle" will help to show the way in which the boy-poet's defining of the word "death" is not as complete as has been suggested and thus that his maturity as a poet is not fully attained at the end of the poem.

In the opening, introductory stanza, the mature poet begins reflecting on his experience as a boy. He concludes: "I . . ./ A reminiscence sing." In this stanza, composed of a single sentence, the narrator speaks in a distinct voice, giving a strong sense of the mature poet's knowledge and the way in which it differs from the boy-poet's knowledge. The imagery of the first few lines suggests the mature poet's knowledge of immortality as he sings of the "endlessly rocking" cradle, symbolic of constant birth and thus re-birth, and of the "Ninth-month," symbolic of both birth (the gestation period) and death (September and thus autumn). The poet emphasizes the merging of birth and death in "the sterile sands and the fields beyond" of the next line, again suggesting an association of death and life. These opening lines, which bring together not only death and life but death in life (the month of birth, perhaps of the endlessly rocking cradle, occurs in autumn), suggest the mature poet's awareness of immortality.

The next section of the introductory stanza introduces the subject matter of the reminiscence, the poet's experience as a boy with the bird and the sea. Significantly, the images that were joined in the opening lines to suggest immortality, such as the "sterile sands" and the living "fields," are now separated as the mature poet reflects on himself as a boy. He begins "Out from the patches of briers and blackberries" and concludes twelve lines later with "Throwing myself on the sand." The initial description of his boyhood experiences hints at the many images that will be repeated later in the body of the poem, but just as the youth does not fully understand the implications of the messages he receives from the bird and the sea, the various meanings of these images are not yet fully apparent to the reader. Only upon completing the poem, and thus only in retrospect, can the reader assign significance to these descriptions. The introductory stanza concludes with an emphasis on the poet's status as "A man" who is the "uniter of here and hereafter."

—A. James Wohlpart, "From Outsetting Bard to Mature Poet: Whitman's 'Out of the Cradle' and the Sea-Drift Cluster," *Walt Whitman Review* 10, no. 4 (December 1964): pp. 77–79.

BEVERLY STROHL ON LOSS AND RECOVERY OF THE SELF

[In the excerpt below, Beverly Strohl discusses the significance of the title and the imagery of the first section of the poem in terms of the loss and eventual recovery of the self.]

'Out of the Cradle Endlessly Rocking' is a poem that symbolically presents to us the dissipation and projection of self and eventual re-unification of self that the romantic personality was continually undergoing. The movement from a negative to a positive romantic state was characterized often by definite feelings of loss of self and re-structuring of a new self, but this process was not unique with this over-all pattern alone. Continually the romantic had to re-define his role because his orientation was useful only temporarily. The romantic, aware as he was of the organic nature of life, had to break down his orientation once it had been fully realized because he knew it was a tragic mistake to regard as final an achieved orientation at one point in his life. The romantic is aware that value, identity, and order are experienced only temporarily in moments of illumination. The self as it emerges does not do so through a perception of order and value in the world; rather, order and value emerge from the perception of self. Therefore, nature is not the source of value, but the occasion for projecting it.

The 'cradle endlessly rocking' metaphorically reveals the eternal movement from disorientation to orientation and *vice versa*. Not only does man rock back and forth in a succession of lives and deaths, but within his life he rocks back and forth in a succession of roles and identities. This basic image of the title, and more importantly of the first line, creates for us a sense of movement that is important to the poem as a whole. The notion of organicism, or the vital and continual unfolding of all things, should intimate to us a perpetual motion of revelation; and this is paralleled in the basic kinetic imagery. The first section alone of the poem has many words and phrases emphasizing this pattern of movement—'shuttle,' 'play of shadows twining and twisting,' 'fitful risings and fallings,' 'myriad,' 'twittering, rising, or overhead passing,' 'borne,' 'hurriedly,' 'throwing,' confronting,' 'taking,' 'swiftly leaping.' The organic concept is repeatedly being underscored in the first section. Whitman indirectly makes a great deal of the organic principle because it is central to his poem.

The image of the sea, so prevalent in the poem, also parallels the rocking of the cradle. Whitman is using the sea as an all-inclusive metaphor for life. Profound, ever changing, encompassing all aspects, and continually moving, it is the flux of life in which the person is placed and on which the self must, in turn, place order.

Along with this, because he is concerned with re-creating for us a particular subconscious event, the imagery is vague and confused and presided over by the 'yellow half-moon,' the denizen of the dark night. A symbolic extension of this would reveal that the dark unconscious of the personality is attempting to suggest its crisis to us. The first section wavers between innocence and understanding, between a real occurrence infused with symbolic meaning and symbolic representation rendered in real terms. The phrase, 'play of shadows,' which presents to us the unreal aspect, is as much at home in this section as 'patches of briers,' which provokes a feeling of a very real and tangible experience. The moon not only suggests to us the motif of the dark unconscious; but because it is so inaccessible, it conveys a notion of transcendent idealism. This idealism needs to come closer to the condition of life in the new orientation that Whitman is trying to achieve.

The cradle image also naturally suggests childhood. In assuming a new orientation the person passes through phases paralleling infancy, youth, and maturity. Whitman is being born into a new orientation as he graphically tells us. 'Out of the ninth-month midnight' means not only that he is trying to place his spiritual occurrence in time and space, but that he is speaking plainly of the fulfillment of gestation and birth in the ninth month. The child that is born leaves his bed or cradle, wandering forth to find his self. In this period that begins the new orientation, because he has not yet had his moment of illumination that would complete his orientation, the world seems 'sterile' and without any meaning. In order to find meaning through an awareness of self, the boy projects his identity by conceptualizing it in something else. Whitman reveals this through his symbolic reminiscence of the mockingbird.

—Beverly Strohl, "An Interpretation of 'Out of the Cradle,'" *Walt Whitman Review* 10, no. 4 (December 1964): pp. 83–84.

SANDRA M. GILBERT ON MALE INDIVIDUATION

[Sandra M. Gilbert is a well-known feminist critic and has written, among other works, *The Madwoman in the Attic: The Woman Writer and the Nineteenth Century Literary Imagination*. She is also one of the editors of *The Norton Anthology of Literature by Women: The Traditions in English*. In the excerpt below, Gilbert discusses Whitman's process toward male individuation in "Out of the Cradle Endlessly Rocking."]

Certainly, if we attempt a moderately close reading of "out of the Cradle," we should be able to perceive rather quickly at least the outlines of the gender-inflected structures that this great ode dramatizes. From beginning to end, after all, Whitman's poem emphasizes not (as Bedient's argument would imply) the speaker's "merging" and "flowing" but his individuation—particularly his separation from "the feminine"—and the priestly (indeed, as George B. Hutchinson has recently observed, the shamanistic) authority that he has gained through such individuation as well as through what, as we shall see, is in essence a kind of "positional" identification with another male singer (the mockingbird) who, as totemic ally, represents a brotherhood of magical, lovelorn *Meistersingers*.

The famously incantatory opening of "Out of the Cradle," for instance, with its long series of clauses in parallel structure, stresses not only the gift *from, up,* and *out* of the seashore that the poet remembers receiving, but also his own separation from the elements of nature, his emergence *out, up* and *from* the mystically maternal forces emblematized by the endlessly rocking cradle of the deep. (Indeed, as several commentators have noted [e.g., Schapiro], the original version of this long shamanistic incantation followed "the musical shuttle" in line 2 with the specifically sexualized phrase, "Out of the boy's mother's womb and from the nipples of her breast."] In addition, as he recalls his empowerment by *and emergence from* the maternal chaos of the natural world, the poet strengthens himself and proclaims his already achieved authority through a frankly arrogant self-definition: "I, chanter of pains and joys, uniter of here and hereafter/Taking all hints to use them, but *swiftly leaping beyond them.*" This opening passage clearly constitutes, as Spitzer long ago pointed out, a "proem, composed in the epic style of [Virgil's great] *arma virumque cano,*" and by prolonging his sentence, accumulating clause after clause, Whitman further reinforces his power. In Spitzer's words, "The longer the sentence, the longer the reader must wait for its subject, the more we sense the feeling of triumph once this subject is reached: the Ego of the poet that dominates the cosmos."

On the surface, the poignant tale of the mockingbirds—the "two feather'd guests from Alabama"—that constitutes the central episode of "Out of the Cradle" and gives rise to the operatic song of loss which dominates that episode would seem in its pathos too domestic, even too sentimental, to follow the heroic Virgilian opening Spitzer describes. Yet as D. H. Lawrence, always one of Whitman's strongest readers, argued many years before Spitzer wrote his essay, this apparently domestic anecdote is really, in the deepest sense, about male bonding. For the disappearance of the "she-bird crouched on her nest"—lost, "May-be kill'd, unknown to her mate"—is essential to the boy's getting of wisdom. As Lawrence put it, "creative life must come near to death, to link up the mystic circuit. The pure warriors must stand on the brink of death. So must the men of a pure creative nation. . . . And so it is . . . where the male bird sings the lost female: *not that she is lost, but lost to him who has had to go beyond her, to sing on the edge of the great sea, in the night.*"

—Sandra M. Gilbert, "Now in a Moment I Know What I Am For," in *Walt Whitman of Mickle Street: A Centennial Collection,* ed. Geoffrey M. Sill (Knoxville: University of Tennessee Press, 1994): pp. 171–72.

Thematic Analysis of
"As I Ebb'd with the Ocean of Life"

"As I Ebb'd with the Ocean of Life," another seashore poem concerned with childhood memories of the sea and the beach, was first listed as Poem No. 1 in the 1860 edition of *Leaves of Grass;* it received its permanent title in 1881. As the title suggests, this is a poem in which Whitman expresses doubts about his poetic achievements; the word "ebb'd," more than the reflux of the tide, represents the poet's depression:

> As the ocean so mysterious rolls toward me closer and closer,
> I too but signify at the utmost a little wash'd-up drift.

At the time he was writing "As I Ebb'd with the Ocean of Life," Whitman was unemployed and clearly questioning his development as a poet. The thrust of this poem is his need to return to his symbolic origins, here the seascape, which he addresses as his parents, "Where the fierce old mother endlessly cries for her castaways." The seascape expresses his feelings of alienation and uprootedness, his anxiety over his bold experimentation with meter and form.

"As I Ebb'd with the Ocean of Life" is divided into four numbered sections, each containing an internal debate over the meaning of the poet's achievement as well as an admonishment from an accusing parent. In the first section, Whitman reexamines his life and work and the reasons for his feelings of isolation; he chastises himself for being overly proud and confident:

> I musing late in the autumn day, gazing off southward,
> Held by this electric self out of the pride of which I utter poems.

In the second section, the poet identifies with the debris washed up on shore, an expression of his mental state:

As I wend the shores I know not,

> As I list to the dirge, the voices of men and women wreck'd,
> As I inhale the impalpable breezes that set in upon me,
> As the ocean so mysterious rolls toward me closer and closer,
> I too but signify at the utmost a little wash'd-up drift,
> A few sands and dead leaves to gather,
> Gather and merge myself as part of the sands and drift.

The internal debate intensifies, incorporating the voices of other poets from whom Whitman has learned his craft. The poet is left with a feeling of extreme emptiness and insignificance. In this stanza, Whitman's use of the word "balk'd" is twofold: first, it describes the poet's obstructed creative situation; second, it describes an argument:

> O baffled, balk'd, bent to the very earth,
> Oppress'd with myself that I have dared to open my mouth,
> Aware now that amid all that blab whose echoes recoil upon me I
> have not once had the least idea who or what I am,
> But that before me all my old arrogant poems the real Me stands yet
> untouch'd, untold, altogether unreach'd,
> Withdrawn far, mocking me with mock-congratulatory signs and
> bows,
> With peals of distant ironical laughter at every word I have written,
> Pointing in silence to these songs, and then to the sand beneath.

His poems are personified as his cruel interlocutors, responding with "peals of distant ironical laughter at every word I have written."

In the third section, Whitman becomes more aggressive. The poet implicates nature for providing the material for his poems:

> You friable shore with trails of debris,
> You fish-shaped island, I take what is underfoot,
> What is yours is mine my father.

Nature must now share the same blame for his bold experimentation with free verse:

> I too have bubbled up, floated the measureless float, and been wash'd
> on your shores,
> I too am but a trail of drift and debris,
> I too leave little wrecks upon you, you fish-shaped island.

For all of these harsh words, the poet still longs for a loving reunion with his surrogate parent:

> Kiss me father,
> Touch me with your lips as I touch those I love,
> Breathe to me while I hold you close the secret of the murmuring I
> envy.

The poet wants the answer to an age-old, jealously guarded secret.

In the fourth stanza, signs of hope and renewal emerge as the poet concedes that his depression will lift: "Ebb, ocean of life, (the flow will return)"; parentheses around the return indicate the unstable nature of this renewed hope, an instability with which Whitman still struggles to overcome:

> I mean tenderly by you all,
> I gather for myself and for this phantom looking down where we
> lead, and following me and mine.

In the end, Whitman redeems his poetry by portraying himself as the gatherer of the ruins of past tradition, a tradition that is gone but still vibrant:

> You up there walking or sitting,
> Whoever you are, we too lie in drifts at your feet. ❀

Critical Views on
"As I Ebb'd with the Ocean of Life"

MELVIN ASKEW ON LYRICAL ASPECTS IN
"AS I EBB'D WITH THE OCEAN OF LIFE"

[In the excerpt, Melvin Askew privileges the lyrical (musical) aspects of the poem over the more conventional emphasis on its biographical contents and, in so doing, highlights the philosophical idealism within the poem.]

Even were it not for the sober lamentation or the grieved acceptance of human confusion and ignorance that characterize 'As I Ebb'd with the Ocean of Life,' the poem would nonetheless be a significant one. Part of its significance, of course, is that in imagery and theme it is closely related to some of the more famous Whitman poems, 'There Was a Child Went Forth' (1855), 'Crossing Brooklyn Ferry' (1856), 'Out of the Cradle Endlessly Rocking' (1858), and 'Song of the Universal' (1874). And again part of its significance is that it is a poetic compendium of Emersonian, idealistic thought, even though the poem itself seems on first reading pessimistic. But curiously, in spite of this dual significance, the lyric has never, according to available bibliographic resources, been treated to full thematic and structural analysis. [. . .]

The structural and thematic principle of 'As I Ebb'd' is in line 15 of stanza 1, 'I thought the old thought of likenesses,' and it is stated as purpose in the quasi-dramatic structure of the poem in the last line of stanza 1, 'As I walk'd with that electric self seeking types.' The poem, then, is about the poet walking alone, 'seeking types' which Paumanok presents to him: 'These you presented to me you fish-shaped island.' And the conduct of the remainder of the poem is the discovery of types and their values to the reader.

The types themselves are idealistic and Emersonian. Emerson believed, briefly and simply, that somewhere outside time and space, pure being was; that the plastic stress of ideality (or pure being) consequently became 'types' of the ideal. This notion, for example, modified the 'shape' of things in time and space; that these things consequently became 'types' of the ideal. This motion, for example, is expressed throughout Emerson's early essays, but more importantly it is in part the burden of 'The Poet' and it largely comprises the theme of Emerson's own fairly bad poem, 'Each and All.' But further, Emerson believed that the idea was so pure, so complete and whole in itself, that each one contained within itself the viture of all idea(s); therefore, he thought, all ideas are contained in each type and each type represents all ideas. And this notion, as we will see, is fundamental to the unity of 'As I Ebb'd.'

The validation of the close relationship between Emersonian doctrine and the theme and subject of 'As I Ebb'd' is in the following lines:

> Held by this electric self out of the pride of which I utter poems,
> [I] was seiz'd by the spirit that trails in the lines underfoot,
> The rim, the sediment that stands for all the water and all the land of the globe.

The crucial phrase here is *stands for,* and the meaning is obviously that the 'rim' and the sediment are metaphors or types; they stand for something, namely, all the land and all the water of the globe. This sediment in stanza 1, then, is a type for all things, and appearing as 'lines underfoot' and 'slender windrows,' it furnishes the fundamental and unifying image of the entire poem; it is the prototype, the form, or 'type' that the poet finds everywhere he looks. [...]

The poet himself 'signifies' or 'stands for' something like the sands drifted by sea and land, and 'sediment' and speaker are then both poets and poems. But more specifically still, the function of the speaker as poet is identified with the function of land and sea (which then becomes a process of poetry). The 'real Me' stands aside, points 'in silence to these songs, and then to the sand beneath,' and equates the two, sands, songs, lines, or slender windrows. One, that is to say, is a type of the other, and they are both the same thing—poems, metaphors.

In stanza 3, the post reiterates the patterns of types established so far:

> You oceans both, I close with you.
> We murmur alike reproachfully rolling sands and drift, knowing not why,
> These little shreds indeed standing for you and me and all. [...]

We, all human, are poems, as it were, of God. Indeed, in the structure of the poem, man is a type of God even as God, like man, the-sea-and-the-land, and the speaker, is a Poet.

The conception of the poem is melodramatic, in part because a philosophical system which distinguishes ideal from actual presupposes melodrama. The principal agents of the poem, or more accurately, all the *things* in the poem which are presented as poem (or type) producers, are themselves divided into two opposing parts. But each 'poet' is ultimately identified with the others because the opposing parts of each demonstrate the same characteristics. At the very outset of the poem, the sea is distinguished from the land; the one is identified with mother, the other with father; the joining of the two results in the poet, on the one hand, and in a type of poetry, on the other, the slender windrows and drift. Similarly, the poet is bifurcated into the me or the 'I' and the 'real Me' or the 'electric self.' And the joining of the two produces the poems which are analogous to the 'lines' that trail underfoot. And finally, God is bifurcated inasmuch as He is *in* Himself and also *in* the types, the people, the 'men and women wreck'd' who lie in drifts at His feet. [. . .]

No poem, however, earns its stature and greatness simply by the integrity of its structure or the necessity of its language and form. Many relatively trivial literary works can exhibit the same or at least analogous virtues. The durability and greatness of a poem, on the contrary, depend largely on the success with which the poet assimilates the imagined or actual facts of life and organizes them within intelligible, significant, and ultimately relevant patterns in such a way that personal and peculiar values become typical and universal values. Here, it seems, lies the greatness of 'As I Ebb'd with the Ocean of Life.'

—Melvin Askew, "Whitman's 'As I Ebb'd with the Ocean of Life,'" *Walt Whitman Review* 10, no. 4 (December 1964): pp. 87–91.

GAY WILSON ALLEN AND CHARLES T. DAVIS
ON THE SYMBOLISM OF WHITMAN'S FATHER

[Gay Wilson Allen and Charles T. Davis are both eminent Whitman scholars. In this excerpt from their book, *Walt Whitman's Poems,* they discuss the symbolism of "As I Ebb'd with the Ocean of Life" in terms of Whitman's father and the circumstances involving his lost editorship at the time the poem was written.]

Considered without regard to Whitman's biography, this poem is an allegory (perhaps the most definitely allegorical of all his poems) in which the poet finds exact analogies between the two oceans ("You oceans both"), the "ocean of life" and the physical ocean. Just as the ocean has its ebb and flow, its calms and storms, and casts up debris onto the shore, so does mortal life have its vicissitudes, and man is so controlled by forces beyond his puny strength that he often seems little more than flotsam himself. [. . .]

In the depths of his discouragement ... the poet walked the shore of Long Island in the late afternoon one autumn day—an appropriate time and season for his mood. He had written the poems of his first two editions out of what he conceived to be the pride of man in himself and more specifically out of his own pride in his apparent health and strength, moral and physical. But now, as a failure, he feels a kinship with the slender winrows cast up by the ocean. It seems to him that he too has been battered by some mighty force and is as helpless and useless as the sand and drift at his feet. He wonders how a man who has so egregiously failed could ever have dared to open his mouth, have attempted to write poems at all.

Yet in his introspection it seems to him that it has not been his inmost self that has failed, his "real Me," but some superficial part of himself. This super Ego seems to stand aside and mock and deride him "With peals of distant ironical laughter at every word I have written." He is now completely humbled, and in the spirit of humility—not despair but genuine intellectual humility—he is aware of his ignorance. He has not "really understood any thing, not a single object," and, perhaps in unconscious self-justification, he adds that "no man ever can." But he is not cynical or bitter. He still wants to understand both oceans, and his humility gives him a new appreciation for his native island (everyday life?), which he symbolizes by "my father."

Walter Whitman, Sr., was himself a failure in life, a blunt, hardworking, unlucky man who had little aptitude for business or the usual methods of getting ahead in the world. In this poem, however, the "father" is only partly and indirectly Walter Whitman, Sr.; he symbolizes the land, the physical realm, as distinguished from the realm of spirit, from which all souls emerge into mortality. The ocean, therefore, is the "mother," who moans for her unfortunate children, the "castaways." From the "father" the poet begs an affectionate kiss and some intimation of the meaning of the murmuring of the ocean, which is to say the meaning of existence, the purpose of life.

Section 4 is an invocation to the "fierce old mother." The poet asks her to continue her moaning but not to deny him or be angry with him: "I mean tenderly by you and all." He is, he thinks, greedy in his ambitions; he combs the beach only for himself and "this phantom looking down where we lead. . ." What is the "phantom"? The poet's soul or super Ego, which stands far off and mocks him in his failure.

The poet and his poems ("Me and mine. . .") are themselves no more than the froth and bubbles and sea-drift cast up by the ocean of life, "Buoy'd hither from many moods, one contradicting another," and "we too lie in drifts at your feet." This is Whitman's apology in 1859–1860 for his life and his poems. But he is not entirely without hope for the future, for he began his invocation (Section 4), "Ebb, ocean of life, (the flow will return,)." Though he does not state his confidence in the return of his own "flow," we may assume that he has such hope, for after the "ebb" must inevitably come the "flow"; such is the law of both oceans. Perhaps the very act of writing the poem marked the turn of the tide. It is significant that the first line of the poem (which gave the permanent title) uses the past tense.

—Gay Wilson Allen and Charles T. Davis, *Walt Whitman's Poems: Selections with Critical Aids* (New York: New York University Press, 1955): pp. 192–94.

[Paul Zweig is the author of *Walt Whitman: The Making of
the Poet, The Heresy of Self-Love,* and *Three Journeys.* In the
excerpt below from his biography, Zweig discusses
Whitman's achievement in the poem "As I Ebb'd with the
Ocean of Life" as a fierce acceptance of a failed relationship
with his father.]

These were shaky years. The feelings bared by the "Calamus" poems
were probably part of it. Whitman did not know who he was any
more. If not America's "giant," then who? Maybe the lone boy
without friends; the job-hopping and house-hopping young man;
the failure who, like his father, had a stubborn, angry streak that
often brought his professional activities to nought. Whitman had
fought off his father—borne him, dead, from the house. He had
tried to edit out of his poems, and out of his personality as well, the
angers, the paralyzing glooms. To his brothers and sisters, and to
America entire, he wanted to be the father whose lack obsessed him:
not an angry, helpless father, but a benign magnetic one, potent,
serene; "the good grey poet." But now the failure was there, and this
time Whitman did not turn away. In an odd way, father and failure
went together for Whitman, giving rise now to a remarkable poem,
which he published in the new *Atlantic Monthly,* in April 1860—one
of his few legitimate publications of these years—under the title
"Bardic Symbols," later "As I Ebbed with the Ocean of Life."

The poem opens with the poet walking on a Long Island beach.
The tide is out, and the wet sand near the water is strewn with
"lines" of *debris:*

> chaff, straw, splinters of wood, weeds, and the sea gluten,
> Scum, scales from shining rocks, leaves of salt lettuce, left by the tide.

Here, indeed, are "symbols," or, should we say "tokens"? But, unlike
the tokens he had plucked for his lovers in "These I Singing in
Spring," they stand here for deflated hope, failed poems, abandon-
ment. They have been stranded by the ocean, that "fierce old
mother":

> a little washed up drift,
> A few sands and dead leaves to gather.

As always, Whitman's drama of experience is expressed in metaphors of poetry. He wrote about writing because living to him was writing; and writing—poetry—was the root activity of life, as it was for Shelley, Wordsworth, and Blake. Not only is *Leaves of Grass* a "language experiment," its subject, irrepressibly and often surprisingly, is language. In his low spirits, he sees a resemblance between himself and the stranded "lines" at his feet. He, too, is shrunken; his glorious miscellanies have become heapings of debris abandoned by the surges of the inspiriting mother-ocean. The old "twoness," which had haunted Whitman—the watcher peeled from his actions and chilling them with self-doubt; the "twoness" which had been dissolved by the erotic marriage of self and soul in "Song of Myself"— reappears now, in a figure of savage self-mockery:

> O baffled, balked,
> Bent to the very earth, here preceding what follows,
> Oppressed with myself that I have dared to open my mouth,
> Aware now, that, amid all the blab whose echoes recoil upon me, I
> have not once had the least idea who or what I am,
> But that before all my insolent poems the real Me still stands
> untouched, untold, altogether unreached,
> Withdrawn far, mocking me with mock-congratulatory signs and
> bows,
> With peals of distant ironical laughter at every word I have written or
> shall write,
> Striking me with insults till I fall helpless upon the sand.

There is a kind of crazed honesty, a fierce self-acceptance, in this poem. One thinks of Yeats's dirge for the collapse of his creative powers, in "The Circus Animal's Desertion." The scene of the poem is the scene of Whitman's strength: the Long Island beaches of his childhood and early manhood. The sound is the rolling surf he would one day identify with the rolling rhythm of his long lines. But now, ironically, he has no access to that strength. The creative tide has ebbed, stranding at his feet these pitiful tokens of failed language. And now Whitman makes one of those leaps of association that are so improbable, yet so filled with the voice's own authority, that one hears the unconscious at work: a slip of impulse—an inspiration—that suddenly says everything:

> You friable shore, with trails of debris!
> You fish-shaped island! I take what is underfoot;
> What is yours is mine, my father. [. . .]

Kiss me, my father,
Touch me with your lips, as I touch those I love,
Breathe to me, while I hold you close, the secret of the wondrous
    murmuring I envy,
For I fear I shall become crazed, if I cannot emulate it, and utter
    myself as well as it.

Whitman calls upon his father, kisses and implores him. From the scene of his vanished strength, he reaches out, in a brotherhood of failure, to the father he had buried. Buried, in fact, four years earlier; buried, symbolically, when he came home as a young man, to become the central influence in his family; buried, more problematically, in the almost unbroken silence of his poems which, with rare exceptions, never mention any father. Yet here now is his father, come back from the dead, as psychopomp, or spirit guide, a companion of dark moods. The father Whitman had fled in his "gigantism" and his lusty assertions catches up with him. This is the scene that is missing from the Gothic melodrama of his early stories. There the son punished the father, by mutilating himself before his eyes. Here, his hurt has enabled him to see his father as if for the first time, and draw from him a kind of negative strength: the ability to endure and thrive in failure. The poem ends with this note of negative triumph. The "young giant," who had cockily refused to take his hat off, even to God, now accepts his shrunken feelings. He embraces what the religious philosopher Rudolf Otto has called the sentiment of "creatureliness": the crushing conviction of one's own smallness and insignificance before the immensity of God.

—Paul Zweig, *Walt Whitman: The Making of the Poet* (New York: Basic Books, 1984): pp. 306–309.

Thematic Analysis of
"When Lilacs Last in the Dooryard Bloom'd"

"When Lilacs Last in the Dooryard Bloom'd," written in 1865 only weeks after the assassination of Abraham Lincoln on April 15th, is Whitman's tribute to his beloved fallen leader. Composed in sixteen sections, "When Lilacs Last in the Dooryard Bloom'd" begins by establishing its three overriding symbols: lilacs, representing an ever-renewing springtime and a source of consolation; the western star, which symbolizes the fallen president; and the hermit thrush, whose presence in the poem is a reassurance that consolation can be found, as the bird has found its way to express grief through song:

> Death's outlet song of life—(for well, dear brother, I know
> If thou wast not granted to sing thou would'st surely die.)

The poem is written in the form of an elegy, a poem occasioned by the death of an exemplary person (here Lincoln). An elegy includes a ceremonial mourning, a description of the procession of mourners, a song of lament about the person's death and a praising of his virtues, and a consolation for the loss of the deceased. Elegies often have been used for political purposes, as a means of healing the nation; in this instance, Whitman serves as the representative democratic man.

Section 1 sets forth two of the symbols through which the poet expresses his grief: "When lilac's last in the dooryard bloom'd,/ And the great star early droop'd in the western sky." Lilacs are traditionally one of the most popular spring shrubs in American gardens, with their delicate color and lovely fragrance. In stark opposition to their beauty is the poet's grief-stricken, plaintive voice in section 2, in which the eternal promise of spring's renewal is denied to both the poet and the fallen president:

> O great start disappear'd! O the black murk that hides the star!
> O cruel hands that hold me powerless! O helpless soul of me!
> O harsh surrounding cloud that will not free my soul.

Trapped within his own inconsolable emotions, the poet sings in section 3 of the virtues of the lilacs,

tall-growing with heart-shaped leaves of rich green,
With many a pointed blossom, rising, delicate, with the perfume
strong I love,
With every leaf a miracle.

Section 4 introduces the third symbol of the poem, the hermit
thrush, "a shy and hidden bird . . . warbling a song," whose behavior
is like a person in mourning, withdrawing from the world when
overcome with grief. The bird presents the poet with an antidote for
his grief through song, "death's outlet song of life." It now remains
for the poet to learn to sing of his grief; to do so, he must first elicit
the sympathy of nature.

In section 5, nature sympathizes with America's grief, wearing the
garments of mourning as the coffin makes its long journey from
Washington to Springfield, Illinois, where Lincoln is buried:

> Amid the grass in the fields each side of the lanes—passing the end-
> less grass,
> Passing the yellow-spear'd wheat, every grain from its shroud in the
> dark-brown fields uprisen,
> Passing the apple-tree blows of white and pink in the orchards,
> Carrying a corpse to where it shall rest in the grave.

Against this backdrop of a sympathetic natural landscape, sections 6
and 7 hold the ceremonial trappings of a state function, replete with
flags and "crape-veiled women" standing in reverence as the coffin
passes. As the coffin makes its physical journey, the poet makes his
mental journey, to work through his grief and mourning. Whitman
addresses Lincoln's coffin, which "passes through lanes and streets,/
Through day and night, with the great cloud darkening the land," as
a living person with the faculty of knowing and hearing; the poet
thus bestows immortality upon the fallen leader.

In section 8, Whitman replaces this animated coffin with a world
beyond the grave that speaks directly to him:

> O western orb, sailing the heaven,
> Now I know what you must have meant, as a month since we walk'd,
> As we walk'd up and down in the dark blue so mystic,
> As we walk'd in silence the transparent shadowy night,
> As I saw you had something to tell as you bent to me night after
> night.

Whitman understands now the greater meaning of Lincoln's death.

In section 9, the poet pauses to contemplate the soothing voice of the bird:

> O singer bashful and tender! I hear your notes—I hear your call,
> I hear, I come presently, I understand you.

In sections 10 and 11, the poet consigns his love for Lincoln to a beautiful and peaceful chamber, a memory palace, and describes the furnishings that will pay homage to this great man. Whitman is creating through his poem a national monument, with

> Pictures of growing spring and farms and homes,
> With floods of the yellow gold of the gorgeous, indolent, sinking sun,
> burning, expanding the air, . . .
> And all the scenes of life.

In section 12, the mood of lamentation is transformed into a mood of hope and exultation for both the poet and the nation. Nature is in harmony once more with this newfound happiness:

> Lo! the most excellent sun so calm and haughty,
> The violet and purple morn, with just-felt breezes,
> The gentle, soft-born measureless light,
> The miracle, spreading, bathing all—the fulfill'd noon,
> The coming eve, delicious—the welcome night, and the stars,
> Over my cities shining all, enveloping man and land.

In section 13, hope is reborn for the hermit thrush as well; Whitman encourages the bird to "pour your chant from the bushes. . . . Sing on dearest brother—warble your reedy song." The poet is now secure that lilac, star, and thrush are the fulfilled promise of immortality, of death and rebirth. He welcomes the bird's "uttermost woe" by transforming it into a sign of freedom: "O liquid, and free, and tender!/ O wild and loose to my soul—O wondrous singer!"

In section 14, the poet unites the two strands of death—the sacred and the profane—to triumph over the fear of death:

> Then with the knowledge of death as walking one side of me,
> And the thought of death close-walking the other side of me,
> And I in the middle, as with companions, and as holding the hands
> of companions,
> I fled forth to the hiding receiving night.

Now that the poet has learned the sacred knowledge that the bird has always known, he can hear the thrush's song as a symbol of transcendence and can be transported to a world beyond the grave:

> And the charm of the singing rapt me,
> As I held, as if by their hands, my comrades in the night,
> And the voice of my spirit tallied the song of the bird.

In section 15, "lovely and soothing death" is praised and longed for, as the poet relates that he has seen "in my eyes unclosed . . . long panoramas" in which the truth is revealed—that it is not the dead who suffer, but the living who are mournful and afraid:

> I saw battle corpses, myriads of them,
> And the white skeletons of young men—I saw them,
> I saw the debris and debris of all the dead soldiers of the war,
> But I saw they were not as was thought,
> They themselves were fully at rest—they suffer'd not,
> The living remain'd and suffer'd.

The poem ends in section 16 with the consolation that only the living need solace, for the dead are resting peacefully. The poet, given a vision of a world beyond the grave, is at last at peace with himself, having completed his own work of mourning. The poet takes part in the ritual of death and renewal:

> Lilac and star and bird twined with the chant of my soul,
> There in the fragrant pines and cedars dusk and dim. ❁

Critical Views on
"When Lilacs Last in the Dooryard Bloom'd"

HARSHARAN S. AHLUWALIA ON THE PUBLIC
AND PRIVATE SELVES IN "LILACS"

[Harsharan S. Ahluwalia is the author of *Whitman's Idea of the Poet in His Preface 1855 and Democratic Vistas*. In the excerpt below, Ahluwalia discusses the presentation of these two opposing concerns in the first few sections of the poem.]

An examination of 'When Lilacs Last in the Dooryard Bloom'd' exhibits the drama of the psychological struggle between the private self and the public self of the poet, and their hard-won integration.

In 'When Lilacs Last in the Dooryard Bloom'd' Whitman sees Lincoln's death as both a personal loss and a national tragedy. He loved and admired Lincoln greatly, though from a distance; so, his grief at his death is personal. At the same time, the American people who loved Lincoln as their hero and leader also mourn his loss. In order to perform his public role, the speaker has to break the 'hold' of his overpowering private grief. To mediate and to write on behalf of the people, a poet must express their loss and also console them. He should teach them how to transcend their loss by comprehending Lincoln's death and extracting from it the meaning that will preserve his memory as well as make a future possible for them.

As the poem opens, the 'I' is mourning, but the reader does not know the object of his grief. This vagueness focuses the reader's attention on the mourner rather than on the person mourned. In fact, the primary focus throughout the poem is on the speaker and his feelings. Yet, the poem is written from a certain chronological distance: the word 'last' in the clause 'When lilacs last in the dooryard bloom'd' suggests that tragedy which caused the speaker's grief had occurred in the spring and he looks back on his reactions. Moreover, he knows that his grief will return with the spring of every year: 'I mourn'd, and yet shall mourn with ever-returning spring.' So, he must not only control his grief now but also find a method of making the memory of Lincoln more creative.

Whitman "Lilacs," from Walt Whitman Review 23, no. 4 (December 1977): pp. 161-65.

It is in terms of three symbols—the star, the lilac and the bird—that Whitman has presented the speaker's personal grief, his growing acceptance of death, and his effort at becoming a poet-priest who will express the grief of the people and console them. Although these symbols have been endlessly scrutinized by critics, many times the meanings given to them are too limited. A symbol gains significance through the complex associations it accumulates as it is introduced and repeated in a poem; it no longer remains an abstraction or an image. My analysis of the poem delineates the gradual process by which an image acquires an atmosphere of association in the poem.

The object of the speaker's grief remains unidentified in Section 1, but it becomes evident in Section 2 that he mourns the 'powerful western fallen star.' In the vague lament, the focus is still on the speaker. Repetition of the 'O' poetically emphasizes the pain he feels, and even conveys his physical cry. By the end of the section, he really begins to lament his own grief:

> O cruel hands that hold me powerless—O helpless soul of me!
> O harsh surrounding could that will not free my soul.

His grief paralyzes him and he must release his soul if he is to be creative.

The instruments of the release of the poet's soul, and therefore of poetic expression appear in Sections 3 and 4. In the description of the lilacs, the color-imagery shifts from 'the black murk' to 'delicate-colored blossoms and heart-shaped leaves of rich green,' and the rhythm of the section quickens accordingly. Realizing resurrection in nature, the speaker comes out of his paralysis and commits his first external 'action': 'A sprig with the flower I break.' After an objective presentation of lilacs, the emphasis again falls on himself. In fact, this sequence patterns the next few sections: the speaker makes forays into the world of nature and life, but then returns again to an awareness of his own grief, about which he makes various statements.

The speaker understands the grief of the bird whose heart (he knows) would burst if he were not gifted to sing. He realizes that 'Death's outlet song of life' sung by the thrush comes from his 'bleeding throat.' This is an important perception in the context of the poem. The speaker and the bird are both singers and have the same problem: how to create and sing in spite of tragedy and loss.

—Harsharan S. Ahluwalia, "The Private Self and the Public Self in Whitman's 'Lilacs,'" *Walt Whitman Review* 23, no. 4 (December 1977): pp. 166–68.

[Jeffrey Steele is the author of *The Representations of the Self in the American Renaissance* and *Unfolding the Mind: The Unconscious in American Romanticism and Literary Theory*. In this excerpt, Jeffrey Steele discusses Whitman's work of mourning in Freudian terms.]

According to James E. Miller, Jr., "When Lilacs Last in the Dooryard Bloom'd" depicts an emotional rehabilitation which involves Whitman's intuitive realization of immortality, his awakening sense that death "paradoxically bestows . . . a rebirth into a spiritual life." But to the extent that this rebirth is viewed as the eternal life which awaits the dead, attention is drawn away from the Poet's progressive re-engagement with sensuous reality. The western star, for example, is allegorized into a sign of immortality—a reading which obscures its functioning within the Poet's self-dramatization. In contrast to Miller's reading, let us examine how the poetic framing of sense impressions stages a psychic drama in which inarticulate grief metamorphoses into self-aware mourning. In this view, the Poet's grief-work consists of a series of operations which ritually reappropriate the world, a world now tinged with a sense of death.

Freud's analysis of mourning in "Mourning and Melancholia" clarifies this process. In his terms, grief is characterized by a "clinging" to the lost object, by the continued investment of psychic energy in the dead. At first, the bereaved loses "interest in the outside world," focusing solely upon the lost object and associated memories. The "work of mourning" necessitates the freeing of this bound energy so that the ego can become "uninhibited again." Over the course of time, "mourning impels the ego to give up the object by declaring the object to be dead and offering the ego the inducement of continuing to live." Eventually, the ego succeeds "in freeing its libido from the lost object." According to this analysis, mourning focuses more upon the obscuring and resurrection of the "soul," than upon the transfiguration of the "dead object."

Turning to Whitman's "Lilacs," we observe that the Poet has lost a part of himself. The "powerful western fallen star," obscured by a "black murk," indicates Lincoln's engulfment by death, but also the Poet's own emotional fixation. His idealized self-image—the star—

had been invested in Lincoln as its fullest embodiment. When Lincoln died, that part of the Poet's soul which had been identified with Lincoln was eclipsed and sank down into the darkness. His task is to recover that lost piece of himself—to regain control of the psychic energy fixated in the lost object. As it is released, that energy will fuel the mourning which lies before him. [. . .]

Whitman's elegy begins with the sense that time has slowly started to move again. The opening lines establish a pattern of imagery which functions within human time as a memorial:

> When lilacs last in the dooryard bloom'd,
> And the great star early droop'd in the western sky in the night,
> I mourn'd, and yet shall mourn with ever-returning spring.

The Poet starts to clarify the formless dusk of grief by associating it with a specific season detached from the temporal flow: spring shall be the time of mourning. Both lilacs and western star gain their meaning from the temporal context of mourning. They are placed within the dramatic framework of elegy so that the Poet can manipulate them as signs of grief—thus objectifying his grief-work. "Now I know what you must have meant," the Poet affirms of the star; the process of temporal ordering makes sense out of the previously undefined chaos of grief. Circumscribing grief by identifying it with specific moments in time, the Poet gains control over his emotional environment. In the process, his dark cloud begins to shrink into a tractable image.

Instead of finding consolation in the immortality of the soul, the Poet is ultimately consoled by his ability to manipulate a series of images which focus the process of poetic grief-work. As Charles Feidelson explains, Whitman's "symbols behave like characters in a drama, the plot of which is the achievement of a poetic utterance." By articulating images around which his pent-up feelings can crystallize, he will establish the ritual dedication of poetry to death. Accordingly, the acts of placing a sprig of lilac upon the passing coffin and of bestowing "gifts" (poetic images) upon the "burial-house of him I love" reassert a creative power tinged by the "black murk" which has enveloped his soul. This reorientation of poetry to the emotional demands of elegy allows the recovery of music and light out of the dark recesses of the self. From imprisoned grief, there will be the release into perception "fresh as the morning," vital as the wind dappling "the breast of the river." F. O. Matthiessen has suggested that "Whitman's greatest act of pioneering was in helping the modern sensibility feel at home in the natural world." In these terms, the dramatic unfolding of this elegy enacts the reappropriation of a sensuous world in which the Poet might dwell if he is able to reframe his voice, re-keying it to the somber tones of mortality.

—Jeffrey Steele, "Poetic Grief-Work in Whitman's 'Lilacs,'" *Walt Whitman Quarterly Review* 2, no. 3 (Winter 1984): pp. 10–12.

※

Justin Kaplan on the Influence of Nature Writing in "Lilacs"

[Justin Kaplan is the author of *Mr. Clemens and Mark Twain, The Language of Names,* and *Walt Whitman: A Life.* In the excerpt below, from his biography of Walt Whitman, Kaplan discusses the influence of the nature writer John Burroughs on Whitman's poetry, specifically, on "When Lilacs Last in the Dooryard Bloom'd." Kaplan discusses the poem as Whitman's farewell song to his creative powers.]

Through [Elijah] Allen he had met an admirer of some years' standing, the young nature writer John Burroughs, then a clerk at the Treasury Department. He came almost daily for breakfasts or dinners with Burroughs and his wife, Ursula, in their little brick house behind the Capitol, on the site of one of the present Senate office buildings—in Burroughs' time the tract also accommodated a potato patch and a cow. "If that is not the face of a poet, then it is the face of a god," Burroughs said soon after he first met Whitman in 1863; three years later he was writing a biographical study, *Notes on Walt Whitman as Poet and Person.* "He reminds one of the first men, the beginners," Burroughs wrote, "has a primitive, outdoor look—not so much from being in the open air as from the texture and quality of his make—a look as of the earth, the sea, or the mountains." But for Burroughs, this same force of raw nature also possessed an enormous gentleness and affection. "There is something indescribable in his look, in his eye—as in that of the mother of many children." [...]

Burroughs, who in the summer of 1865 had just come back from a woodland vacation, was thinking and talking mainly about birds, in particular, the gray-brown hermit thrush. He claimed that even Audubon, who had ignited his lifelong passion for ornithology, had not got this one quite right. The hermit thrush's clear, flutelike, deliberate song—Burroughs rendered it in print as "O spheral, spheral! . . . O holy, holy!"—was "the finest sound in nature," "perhaps more of an evening than a morning hymn . . . the voice of that calm, sweet solemnity one attains to in his best moments." In mid-September, Burroughs noted that Whitman had been "deeply interested in what I tell him of the Hermit Thrush, and he says he has largely used the information I have given him in one of his principal poems."

"Sings oftener after sundown . . . is very secluded . . . likes shaded, dark places," Whitman wrote in one of his improvised notebooks. "His song is a hymn . . . in swamps—is very shy . . . never sings near the farm houses—never in the settlement—is the bird of the solemn primal woods & of Nature pure & holy." That summer, with a sustained inspiration and sureness of word and design he had not known since "Out of the Cradle Endlessly Rocking," he wrote his great elegy for Abraham Lincoln:

> When lilacs last in the dooryard bloom'd,
> And the great star early droop'd in the western sky in the night,
> I mourn'd, and yet shall mourn with ever-returning spring.

"Retrievements out of the night," memories of the dead President fused with the western star Whitman had marveled at the winter skies; the bugle notes he heard coming up out of the night silence and sounding "Lights Out" fused with the voice of the hermit thrush.

> Solitary the thrush,
> The hermit withdrawn to himself, avoiding the settlements,
> Sings by himself a song.
>
> Song of the bleeding throat.

In a critical essay published in 1866, Burroughs said that the rhythms and harmonies of "Lilacs" as well as its method ("a constant interplay—a turning and re-turning of images and sentiments") could best be understood through "the analogy of music." Swamp-wild like the hermit thrush's, Whitman's music also derived from opera and oratorio. "Art-singing and Heart-singing," as he distinguished them twenty years earlier, had become synonymous. Like

Milton's "Lycidas," Shelley's "Adonais," and other great occasional poems, Whitman's farewell to Abraham Lincoln, "the sweetest, wisest soul of all my days and lands," transcends its occasion—Lincoln is never mentioned in it either by name or by office. But "Lilacs" is also an unconscious farewell to the creative powers of an "elderly, literary gentleman" who had said he expected to "range along the high plateau of my life & capacity for a few years now, & then swiftly descend." With the hermit thrush's carol, Whitman again came to terms

> with the knowledge of death as walking one side of me,
> And the thought of death close-walking the other side of me.

When he placed on Lincoln's coffin his symbolic sprig of lilac in flower, "every leaf a miracle," he looked ahead to his own tomb in Harleigh Cemetery. [...]

In its Tennysonian sonority and sweetness of diction even the great "Lilacs" shares with "O Captain" and other poems in *Drum-Taps* a denaturing tendency, signs of retreat from the idiomatic boldness and emotional directness of Whitman's earlier work. Trowbridge felt that the "stock 'poetical' touches" Whitman had taken such care to write out of *Leaves of Grass* were now being deliberately written into *Drum-Taps*, for example, in the manuscript lines,

> lo, in these hours supreme,
> No poem proud, I chanting bring to thee.

—Justin Kaplan, *Walt Whitman: A Life* (New York: Simon and Schuster, 1980): pp. 307–310.

CHARLES FEIDELSON, JR., ON THE ELEGIAC TRADITION

[Charles Feidelson, Jr., is the author of *Symbolism and American Literature* and *Interpretations of American Literature*. In the excerpt below, Feidelson discusses the poem within the context of the elegiac tradition and locates the true subject of the poem to be Whitman himself.]

The patent symbols of Whitman's best poem, "When Lilacs Last in the Dooryard Bloom'd," are conditioned by the thoroughgoing symbolism of his poetic attitude. As in most elegies, the person mourned is hardly more than the occasion of the work; but this poem, unlike *Lycidas* or *Adonias*, does not transmute the central figure merely by generalizing him out of all recognition. Lincoln is seldom mentioned either as a person or as a type. Instead, the focus of the poem is a presentation of the poet's mind at work in the context of Lincoln's death. If the true subject of *Lycidas* and *Adonias* is not Edward King or John Keats but the Poet, the true subject of Whitman's "Lilacs" is not the Poet but the poetic process. And even this subject is not treated simply by generalizing a particular situation. The act of poetizing and the context in which it takes place have continuity in time and space but no particular existence. Both are "ever-returning"; the tenses shift; the poet is in different places at once; and at the end this whole phase of creation is moving inexorably forward.

Within this framework the symbols behave like characters in a drama, the plot of which is the achievement of a poetic utterance. The spring, the constant process of rebirth, is threaded by the journey of the coffin, the constant process of death, and in the first section it presents the poet with twin symbols: the perennially blooming lilac and the drooping star. The spring also brings to the poet the "thought of him I love," in which the duality of life and death is repeated. The thought of the dead merges with the fallen star in Section 2; the thought of love merges with the life of the lilac, from which the poet breaks a sprig in Section 3. Thus the lilac and the star enter the poem not as objects to which the poet assigns a meaning but as elements in the undifferentiated stream of thoughts and things; and the spring, the real process of becoming, which involves the real process of dissolution, is also the genesis of poetic vision. The complete pattern of the poem is established with the advent of the bird in the fourth section. For here, in the song of the thrush, the lilac and star are united (the bird sings "death's outlet song of life"), and the potentiality of the poet's "thought" is intimated. The song of the bird and the thought of the poet, which also united life and death, both lay claim to the third place in the "trinity" brought by spring; they are, as it were, the actuality and the possibility of poetic utterance, which reconciles opposite appearances.

The drama of the poem will be a movement from possible to actual poetic speech, as represented by the "tallying" of the songs of the poet and the thrush. Although it is a movement without steps, the whole being implicit in every moment, there is a graduation of emphasis. Ostensibly, the visions of the coffin and the star (Sections 5 through 8) delay the unison of poet and bird so that full actualization is reserved for the end of the poem. On the other hand, the verse that renders the apparition of the coffin *is* "death's outlet song of life." The poetic act of evoking the dark journey is treated as the showering of death with lilac:

> Here, coffin that slowly passes,
> I give you my sprig of lilac . . .
> Blossoms and branches green to coffins all I bring,
> For fresh as the morning, thus would I chant a song for you,
>   O sane and sacred death.

—Charles Feidelson, Jr., "Symbolism in 'When Lilacs Last in the Dooryard Bloom'd,'" in *Critics on Whitman*, ed. Richard H. Rupp (Coral Gables: University of Miami Press, 1968): pp. 66–68.

Works by
Walt Whitman

Leaves of Grass, ten editions. (1855–1892)

Democratic Vistas. (1870)

Works about
Walt Whitman

Adams, Richard P. "Whitman's 'Lilacs' and the Tradition of Pastoral Elegy." *PMLA* 72 (June 1957): 449–487.

Allen, Gay Wilson. *The Solitary Singer: A Critical Biography of Walt Whitman.* New York: Macmillan, 1995.

———, ed. *Walt Whitman Abroad: Critical Essays from Germany, Scandinavia, France, Russia, Italy, Spain, Latin American, Israel, Japan and India.* Syracuse, N.Y.: Syracuse University Press, 1955.

———. *Walt Whitman as Man, Poet and Legend.* With a checklist of Whitman publications 1945–1960, by Evie Allison Allen. Carbondale, Ill.: Southern Illinois University Press, 1961.

Asselineau, Roger. *The Evolution of Walt Whitman: The Development of a Personality.* Cambridge, Mass.: Harvard University Press, 1960.

———. *The Evolution of Walt Whitman: The Creation of a Book.* Cambridge, Mass.: Harvard University Press, 1962.

Bailey, John C. *Walt Whitman.* New York: Macmillan, 1926.

Bradley, Sculley. "The Fundamental Metrical Principle in Whitman's Poetry," *American Poetry* 10 (January 1939): 437–459.

Chase, Richard. *Walt Whitman Reconsidered.* New York: William Sloan, 1955.

Clifton, Joseph Furness. *Walt Whitman's Workshop.* Cambridge: Harvard University Press, 1928.

Cmiel, Kenneth. *Democratic Eloquence: The Fight over Popular Speech in Nineteenth-Century America.* New York: Morrow, 1990.

Daiches, David. "Walt Whitman as Innovator." In *The Young Rebel in American Literature,* ed. Carl Bode. London: Heinemann, 1959.

———. "Walt Whitman: Impressionist Prophet." In *Leaves of Grass One Hundred Years After,* ed. Milton Hindus. Palo Alto: Stanford University Press, 1955.

De Selincourt, Basil. *Walt Whitman: A Critical Study.* London: Martin Secker, 1914.

Dressman, Michael Rowan. "Walt Whitman's Plans for the Perfect Dictionary." In *Studies in the American Renaissance*, ed. Joel Myerson. Boston: Twayne, 1979.

Drinnon, Richard. *Facing West: The Metaphysics of Indian-Hating and Empire Building*. New York: Meridian, 1980.

Faner, Robert D. *Walt Whitman and Opera*. Philadelphia: University of Pennsylvania Press, 1951.

Fauset, Hugh l'Anson. *Walt Whitman: Poet of Democracy*. London: Jonathan Cape, 1942.

Folsom, Ed. *Walt Whitman's Native Representations*. New York: Cambridge University Press, 1994.

Furness, Clifton Joseph. "Walt Whitman Looks at Boston." *New England Quarterly* 1 (1928): 353–70.

Gilbert, George. *Photography: The Early Years*. New York: Harper & Row, 1980.

Holloway, Emory. *Whitman: An Interpretation in Narrative*. New York: Knopf, 1926.

Jarrell, Randall. "Some Lines from Whitman." *Poetry and the Age*. New York: Knopf, 1953.

Kaplan, Justin. *Walt Whitman: A Life*. New York: Simon & Schuster, 1980.

Lawrence, D. H. *Studies in Classic American Literature*. New York: Boni & Liveright, 1923.

Lewis, R. W. B., ed. *The Presence of Walt Whitman*. New York: Columbia University Press, 1962.

Miller, Edwin Haviland, ed. *The Artistic Legacy of Walt Whitman*. New York: New York University Press, 1970.

Miller, James E., Jr. *A Critical Guide to "Leaves of Grass."* Chicago: University of Chicago Press, 1957.

Orvell, Miles. *The Real Thing: Imitation and Authenticity in American Culture, 1880–1940*. Chapel Hill: University of North Carolina Press, 1989.

Pearce, Roy Harvey. *The Continuity of American Poetry*. Princeton: Princeton University Press, 1961.

Pollak, Georgiana. "The Relationship of Music to 'Leaves of Grass.'" *College English* 15 (April 1954): 384–394.

Spigelman, Julia. "Walt Whitman and Music." *South Atlantic Quarterly* 41 (April 1942): 167–176.

Stovall, Floyd. *The Foreground of Leaves of Grass.* Charlottesville: University Press of Virginia, 1974.

Swayne, Mattie. "Whitman's Catalogue Rhetoric." *University of Texas Studies in English* 21 (1941): 162–178.

Swinton, William. *Rambles Among Words: Their Poetry, History and Wisdom.* New York: Charles Scribner, 1859.

Trachtenberg, Alan. *The Incorporation of America: Culture and Society in the Gilded Age.* New York: Hill, 1982.

Triggs, Oscar Lovell. "The Growth of 'Leaves of Grass.'" In *The Complete Writings of Walt Whitman.* Camden edition. Richard Maurice Bucke, Thomas B. Harned, and Horace L. Traubel, eds. 10 vols. New York and London: G. Putnam's Sons, 1902.

Ware, Lois. "Poetic Conventions in Leaves of Grass." *Studies in Philology* 81 (January 1929): 47–57.

Waskow, Howard J. *Whitman: Explorations in Form.* Chicago: University of Chicago Press, 1966.

Weathers, Willie T. "Whitman's Poetic Translations of His 1855 Preface." *American Literature* 19 (March 1947): 21–40.

Zweig, Paul. *Walt Whitman: The Making of the Poet.* New York: Basic Books, 1984.

Index of
Themes and Ideas